Preface

The primary aim of this short essay on socialism is to suggest some perspectives in interpretation which readers interested in the subject may find helpful. It is cast in the broad framework of a survey of socialist ideas and the development of modern socialist movements, but its chief concern is not with historical description. On this count, to be sure, it falls far short of comprehensiveness, since it bypasses a number of issues and leaves many a corridor in the edifice of socialism unexplored. However, it makes an attempt to develop a few basic themes and elucidate the logic of socialist ideas: the perspectives thus gained may, I hope, serve as stimulants to further reading. A short bibliography of general and historical works is appended at the end; here the criteria of selection were interpretive interest and breadth of information. I wish to record my thanks to several people: former teachers, students, colleagues and friends, who discussed with me some of the problems raised in this essay. In particular I owe gratitude to Robert Benewick and John Saville for making extensive and valuable comments on the first draft. For all remaining faults as well as the opinions expressed in the essay I am solely responsible. Miss Joan Walton typed the final draft with speed and efficiency. Two points on references: italics in direct quotes always refer to the original, unless otherwise stated; dates in brackets refer to first publication or completion of posthumously printed manuscripts.

Hull, August 1974   R. N. B.

Modern Ideologies

SOCIALISM

R. N. Berki
Department of Politics,
University of Hull

J. M. DENT & SONS LTD
LONDON, MELBOURNE AND TORONTO

Printed in Great Britain
by
Biddles Ltd, Guildford, Surrey
for
J. M. Dent & Sons Ltd
Aldine House, Welbeck Street, London

First published 1975
Reprinted 1978

This book is set in 11 on 12 pt Fournier 185

Hardback ISBN 0 460 10721 6
Paperback ISBN 0 460 11721 1

Contents

1 What is Socialism?

We all know, of course, what socialism is. Or so we think. A number of simple notions and phrases immediately spring to the mind. In company with other ideological concepts, socialism has a double reference. On the one hand, it refers to ideals, values, properties of what is often called the socialist 'vision'. On the other hand, it refers to empirical features of social and political institutions which are supposed concretely to embody the vision. On the level of values, adherents to socialism (who usually concentrate on values) will usually give a prompt answer: socialism stands for the values of freedom, equality, community, brotherhood, social justice, the classless society, co-operation, progress, peace, prosperity, abundance, happiness—to mention just the most important ones. Sometimes the value component of socialism is stated negatively: socialists are opposed to oppression, exploitation, inequality, strife, war, injustice, poverty, misery and dehumanization. On the level of institutions, the answer appears even easier. Here adherents and opponents alike (opponents being more interested in institutions than in values) would say that socialism is opposed to the capitalist private enterprise system which it seeks to replace by a system of control over wealth and property and the social supervision or organization of economic activity; this is often summarized in the formula, the 'common' or 'public ownership of the means of production'.

So far so good. But it doesn't take more than a moment's reflection to see that notions and phrases of this kind are quite inadequate for a proper understanding of socialism; they are abstract, laden with emotion and ambiguity. Take, first of all, the list of socialist values. Apart from their plurality, which is itself a major problem, all these values have several and often conflicting definitions. Simply stated, they fail to distinguish socialists from proponents of other ideologies. Who does *not* profess to believe in freedom, justice and prosperity?

Socialism

Who is not *against* oppression, misery and war? Most people who do not look upon themselves as socialists would probably admit that 'equality' is better than 'inequality', 'brotherhood' and 'co-operation' better than enmity. It is then necessary to probe further and to ask what one *means* by these and similar values. But here we come up against another problem. If we start defining values, we might very easily end up with more and sharper distinctions than we intended, this time highlighting the numerous divisions among socialists. By 'equality', for example, some socialists have meant 'equality of opportunity' while others have meant 'equality of remuneration'—the two are very different, of course. By 'freedom' some have meant the liberty to follow one's natural inclinations and to satisfy one's desires, whereas others have meant by freedom to follow one's reason and to strive for self-improvement. 'Happiness', 'progress', 'brotherhood' have also had widely differing interpretations. And we do not fare much better with an institutional definition either. 'Public ownership' as a general formula is too indefinite, too indiscriminate to have any concrete meaning. It can refer to central planning with complete state ownership of resources; to the nationalization of large industrial and financial concerns only; to state shareholding in private enterprise; to co-determination; to public corporations; to decentralized economies; to workers' control; to producers' co-operatives; and so on and so forth. All these and many others have been advocated under the name of 'socialism'. The truth is that the identity of socialism is elusive, and one can sympathize with learned commentators who have turned away with despair from the task of definition. Perhaps not many would go as far as Dr Angelo Rappoport who, listing thirty-nine definitions of socialism in his *Dictionary of Socialism* (1924), simply declares that he still doesn't know what socialism is, but the sentiment and agony are commonly shared.

Is there then no simple way in which order can be created out of chaos? Has socialism no unitary meaning, no concrete identity? There have been a number of approaches to this problem. Many of them, it will be argued here, err by attempting to impose unity on socialism by drawing hard and fast lines of distinction around it and thereby reducing its content. Reduction or reductionism is a tempting tool of analysis, but it unduly impoverishes the subject matter and succeeds only too often in smothering the interest which it ought to be the task of analysis to stimulate. We shall take a very brief look at a few characteristic forms of reductionism and shall then outline our approach.

Reductionism, in broad terms, can be divided into two main kinds, one being 'political' the other 'academic' reductionism.

The political approach signifies strong emotional involvement with socialism. Here we may encounter the *essentialist* departure which fastens on one or another socialist ideal, declaring it alone to be the 'essence' of socialism. Thus it has been asserted that socialism is fundamentally 'about' equality, freedom, social justice, etc. This approach, however, quite apart from deliberately ignoring the vast variety of socialist literature, commits the error of inflating the definition of its supposedly 'essential' value, subsuming all else under it. Secondly, there is the *transcendentalist* approach which recognizes socialist values only, condemning all that has been so far achieved in institutional terms as being a 'distortion' or 'falsification' of the socialist vision. But here obviously intelligibility is gained only at the price of irrelevance, conceptual purity at the price of practical innocence and impotence.

The third and by far the most important kind of political reductionism is the approach from concrete *commitment*. Here, while the double reference of socialism is duly kept in sight, the problem of complexity is solved simply by denying the legitimacy of the 'socialist' label to those whose understanding of socialism is different. It is, in other words, the attempt to narrow down the meaning of socialism to the meaning of a 'true' socialism. The committed writer draws an uncompromising distinction between 'genuine' socialism—his own—and various heresies. The outstanding case here is the running controversy between Marxists and other militants on the one hand, and social democrats of various kinds on the other. The former, from Lenin and Trotsky to Edward Thompson and Ralph Miliband, have accused social democrats of being opportunists and traitors to socialism: they are not socialists, but 'labourists' or liberals in disguise. The latter, from Kautsky and MacDonald to Bruno Kreisky and Irving Howe, have in turn retorted by arguing that Marxists (particularly those in power) negate socialism by the manner of their rule and political methods: they are not socialists, but 'communists' or 'totalitarians' (they are not Left but East, in Guy Mollet's renowned phrase).

A few points should be made about this controversy right now. In the first place, while it may be readily admitted that both Marxists and social democrats are correct in their respective understanding of the doctrines to which they are committed, it does not follow that they are right in *equating* their views with 'socialism' as such. Both opposing

Socialism

views may have internal coherence and both (or one of them, or
neither) may be valid political doctrines supremely relevant to the
needs of modern society. Yet it still does not follow that either should
have an exclusive proprietary right to the name. Socialism—the name,
the concept, the movement—has a long and chequered history. Even
assuming that historical origins are relevant here, one would be at a
loss when asked what particular meaning *today* derives 'legitimately'
from the 'original' understanding of socialism. Clearly nothing follows
from the facts, cited in practically all commentaries, that 'socialism'
in English was first used publicly in 1827 in connection with the Owenite movement, and in French in 1835 in connection with the Saint-
Simonians.

Names in political discourse show themselves notoriously unstable
over time, and this is especially true of ideological concepts like socialism, communism, social democracy and their ilk. A random glance at
a few historical quirks might warn us against word-fetishism. John
Ruskin, for example, proudly called himself a 'communist', while he
repudiated socialism, republicanism and democracy.[1] For H. M.
Hyndman the term 'socialism' denoted mild, wishy-washy, Christian-
liberal do-goodery, while the term 'social democracy' meant for him
militant Marxism.[2] Today, of course, the opposite would be the case.
It was Proudhon, not Marx and Engels, who first called his doctrine
'scientific socialism'. Bakunin at one time led an organization which was
called the 'Alliance for Socialist Democracy'. Marx himself in his youth
dismissed 'communism' as being only an imperfect realization of 'socialism'.[3] Admittedly later Marxian usage became more systematic, though
never becoming entirely free of ambiguity. The *Manifesto* of 1848 is
called 'Communist' and it does not mince words in contemptuously
dismissing 'socialism'. Yet in a later Preface Engels explains this
usage by reference to political exigencies of the mid-century, now
calling the *Manifesto* itself a product of 'socialist literature'.

Obviously it would not do to deny that there are important substantive differences between the views of social democrats and Marxists.
These differences, however, are best seen as occurring within socialism,
rather than between socialism and something else.[5] As regards contemporary usage, the following rough hints will illuminate the issues.
In *political* terms a distinction is often drawn between 'communists'
and 'socialists' with regard to the methods used by each. Communists
are held to be more extreme, more militant than socialists. But this
distinction is difficult to maintain these days when one encounters

groups like the *Socialist Labour League* in Britain or the *Parti socialiste unifié* in France who profess—with some justice—to be more militant and revolutionary than their respective Communist Parties. In *ideological* terms a distinction is usually drawn between 'communism' and 'socialism', in that communism is thought to imply a more radical reorganization of social (especially labour and property) relationships than socialism. But again, as long as socialists subscribe to some form of 'common ownership', and as long as communists emphasize the common ownership of the 'means of production' (as distinguished from personal effects), the intended line of division must remain blurred.

Surely the significant point about the whole controversy is the fact that no agreement can be reached on nomenclature, that diverse groups all lay claim to the same name, that there is acute, unabating rivalry for the proprietorship of socialism. This may suggest—and the point will be taken up below—that the long-sought-after unity or identity of socialism can perhaps be best grasped through the conflict which accompanies its profession and employment. Let us just make one more remark on the approach from commitment. The search for a 'true' socialism in most cases does not end with Marxism or social democracy as such. The intensity of one's commitment tends to be in inverse ratio to one's willingness to admit of legitimate diversity within the creed. The more fervently one believes in socialism, the more narrowly one will tend to define it. One will proceed, say, from Marxism to Marxism-Leninism, and then on to Stalinism or Trotskism or Maoism as the case may be, and from here to the particular and current sectarian interpretations of these, and finally, if one is not careful, arriving at a 'reductio' which is truly 'ad absurdum'. The danger of commitment is ideological solipsism.

Lastly on this count we may mention the *hostile* approach to socialism. This also involves reductionism in that hostile writers often tend to dismiss socialist ideals, noting only the empirical (and of necessity imperfect) achievements and political activities of socialists. Curiously, this kind of reduction will frequently generate indiscriminate inflation of the institutional aspect, when socialism will be made responsible for every kind of crime and blunder. This then becomes what we might call the 'little old lady' approach, after the proverbial old lady who, in fear of her life-savings and learning about socialism from the illustrated weeklies, finds socialists (or communists) under every bed and behind every bush. Here and there, it seems, thinly disguised little old ladies manage to find their way into the worlds of scholarship and ideological debate.

To turn now to 'academic' reductionism, here the distinguishing marks are the absence of intense emotional involvement with socialism and the desire to be fair and objective in one's dealing with the subject. But reductionism still presents a danger. Two approaches deserve here passing comment. Firstly, there is *legalism* which is often encountered in anthologies on socialism, but also in historical and critical monographs. Legalism consists in lexicographical legislation and can be usually recognized by such formulae as 'socialism will be taken here to mean that . . .' or 'for the purposes of this work socialism will be defined as . . .', etc. Now it would not behove us to dismiss this approach out of hand, for it always signifies serious scholarship and genuine concern with the complexity of the subject matter. Nevertheless, stipulative definitions still involve reductionism. Terse and peremptory definitions as well as marathon definitions running into long and involved sentences, with subordinate clauses and qualifications chasing one another, tend to let the identity of socialism slip by, not to mention their proneness to complicate and to obscure instead of the desired clarification.

Secondly, there is *inessentialism* or the *hardheaded* approach which seeks to solve the problem of unity and diversity by simply disposing of it in unceremonious fashion. Is it difficult to define socialism? This is only because we have posed the question wrongly in the first place, assuming that there is an 'essence' or 'substance' to which socialism refers. But, the hardheaded analyst would argue, words do not 'stand for' things; they have only their 'use' and this varies with the context. Socialism thus might mean a great variety of things to different people at different times, and there is no point in looking for a unitary meaning. So why not—as the argument can be pushed further—try to define and study something harder, more tangible, more coherent, like Marxism or English socialism, or even better, the socialism of a single thinker, Saint-Simon, Marx, Proudhon, Ramsay MacDonald, Trotsky, etc.?

This is an intricate philosophical issue and we must confine ourselves to the making of two points in criticism. Inessentialism appears to be based on a fallacy and it leads logically to a dead-end. The fallacy consists in believing that contexts are limited and isolated from one another. Assume, however, that one has thoroughly digested the doctrines of a single thinker, say Saint-Simon or Marx or Robert

Blatchford, knowing fairly well what the individual in question had 'really meant'. Or assume, more pointedly, that one knows inside out the arguments of the first volume of *Capital* or Blatchford's *Merrie England*. The question still to be asked is about the sense in which (or the extent to which) a single writer or a single text propounds 'socialism'. Now the criteria of judging this point, whether or not a writer actually uses the word 'socialism' (Saint-Simon did not), involve the consideration of evidence from the outside as it were, the historian or critic having to go beyond the writer's own world of meanings. There is something like a 'general meaning' in the world at large, an unconfined discourse in which writers are participating, a sense of words up in the air, not to be connected with any single source or intellectual dwelling-place. There seems to be a running dialectical parley between the hard core of statements occurring in black and white in the pages of books and pamphlets, and the softer substance surrounding it: one could not exist and be made intelligible without the other.

Moreover, taking the hardheaded approach seriously one can see that it may easily confront one with insoluble tasks. It is only in comparison with very complex notions like 'socialism' that others, like Marxism or English socialism, appear more coherent and more tangible. On closer reflection they too reveal themselves as being complex and problematic in the highest degree. What is really 'English socialism'? Fabianism? Owenism? The policies of the Labour Party? Even in the case of single authors we find ambiguities, changes, inconsistencies, incipient contradictions: there is on this analysis really no such thing as 'the' socialism of Saint-Simon, Marx or Trotsky. Instead of a coherent, unitary meaning of socialism we find ourselves in the nominalist's *cul de sac*. It will have been seen by now, of course, that inessentialism runs a parallel course to the approach from commitment: both lead to reduction to unintelligibility. The hardheaded approach, one might venture to conclude, is really the deep-freeze version of the search for a 'true' socialism.

Let us then see where we stand. The foregoing critical—and somewhat laconic—notes on various approaches to the study of socialism already pretty well mark out the method which is going to be adopted in this book. But the implications will have to be spelt out more clearly. We have criticized attempts to reduce socialism to one single 'true' body of doctrines or values. And we have argued that it is erroneous to dismiss the identity of socialism on account of the diverse and conflicting views for which the name provides verbal cover. This amounts to asserting not only that all usages are legitimate, but that all those professing themselves to be socialists are in fact participating in the same discussion. And this, in turn, means advancing the thesis that the identity of socialism lies in the irreducible plurality of values and institutions which constitute its area of reference, and in the very problematic character of any attempt to reconcile these into an harmonious totality. And this, again, means that instead of drawing neat pencil-lines, we have to get hold of a brush. Instead of being preoccupied with its circumference, we should try to grasp socialism as a bundle of complex problems, paradoxes, intellectual and political controversies. Socialism is not 'about' equality any more than it is 'about' justice or happiness. Its identity is not revealed in the Marxian texts alone, nor in the Sermon on the Mount, nor in party manifestoes, nor in underground pamphlets and campus graffiti. Socialism is not a single thing, but a range, an area, an open texture, a self-contradiction.

This last term may require a word or two in explanation. By contradiction we mean here that curious quality of complex notions which makes them amenable to analysis into opposed and conflicting tendencies, rendering the notion itself both 'for' and 'against' the same thing, both 'in' and 'out' of the same universe of discourse. This is not as weird as it might seem at first. Complex notions have not one unitary meaning, but a range of meanings. To determine this range we have to identify the two extreme terms, the outer limits within which all other meanings are located. These extremes are united, since they are the limits of the same range; and they are contradictory, since they form the two opposing ends of the spectrum. Now there is of course a whole tradition of philosophizing behind these stark statements, but it is beyond our scope here to argue out the general thesis in full. There is no need, after all; this approach has had many an illustrious advocate.[6] Our concern is socialism, and the method will have to be tested in the concrete, in terms mainly of the stimulation it may provide. Two tasks only will have to be performed. Firstly, instead of merely recognizing the values and institutions of socialism and ordering them randomly, we shall have to sharpen them, push them into *polar tendencies*. Secondly, in analysing socialism we must not lose sight of its double reference: as a complex ideological notion socialism cannot be divided into simple 'atomic' ideas, but only into miniature complexes which obliquely reflect the complexity of the whole. An 'ism', in other words, must be seen to be made up of other 'isms' which are its constituent parts. In the next chapter we shall explain more fully what is meant here. For now, let us just take an overview of what will here be considered as the predominant contradiction of our subject.

Socialism is a living self-contradiction: this seemingly outrageous statement merely signifies the recognition that socialism as a movement and as a system of ideas expresses an inherently ambivalent attitude to the spirit of the modern age. Socialism is both a child of our modern age, its legitimate and perhaps most typical offspring, and at the same time also the intellectual, emotional and political embodiment of the most resolute denial that the spirit of this age has and could have received. On the one hand, socialism is our advance-guard, on the other it is our link with bygone ages. Its eyes are set firmly on the future, yet its strength and appeal issue from the past.

On one side, socialism is the heir to the Renaissance and the Enlightenment, deriving its values from humanism and classical liberalism. It is these values which together make up the spirit of the age: they assert man's independence from any higher being or supernatural agency, his being rooted in this material world where he has to find his own salvation, his character as a natural being who can, must and will work out his happiness in an earthly environment. Individualism in the sense of self-assertion, secularism in the sense of the felt self-sufficiency of human reason and human society, materialism in the sense of seeking happiness and fulfilment in the possession and enjoyment of objects found in nature or extracted by human labour—these are the chief ingredients of the cultural complex of which socialism, on one side, is the most articulate expression. The 'spirit of the age', of course, is again one of those notions which it would be extremely difficult to define with any degree of precision, yet it is one that we can quite easily recognize around us: in the Western world at any rate we breathe it with the air. It is certain that socialism is a part of it, but it is also certain that socialism parts company with the *Zeitgeist* and becomes its most resolute antagonist when the hidden inevitable tendencies of the latter come to the surface—except that socialism does this with a built-in ambivalence. The way in which the spirit of the age seems inexorably to lead is towards greater and greater materialism, the pursuit of material wealth for its own sake; towards ever starker individualism, the ever more selfish pursuit of individual happiness; towards more and more explicit secularism, coming to assert now (if not openly in theory, certainly in practice) the obsolescence of not only religion, but any kind of objective moral standards.

The socialist critique of these modern trends has been of two different kinds. The first is as it were quantitative: it highlights the inadequacy of the material and institutional provisions made by liberal-capitalist society (it is this society where we find the spirit of the age taking flesh) for all its members in terms of its own professed contemporary values. That is to say, if the Enlightenment and classical liberalism, through their great historical instruments, the economic and political revolutions of the eighteenth century, have promised and envisioned individual happiness and the blessings of material progress for *all* men, socialists have pointed out that the outcome was something quite different. The dethronement of monarchs, the curbing of the power of aristocracies, the immense strides made in the improvement of productive techniques, only resulted in a new kind of poverty and misery for the masses. One kind of oppression was replaced by another and possibly more pernicious kind. *Some* men, the new rulers and owners of wealth, reaped the benefits of the changes, while the rest, the great majority, were still excluded from its enjoyment. Classical liberalism and the society which it brought into being were themselves becoming fetters on further progress, preventing the extension of the advances made for the benefit of all members of the human race. Socialism, as the heir to the Enlightenment, was appointed to take over at this point.

Note, however, that this quantitative critique of liberal-capitalist society still takes for granted the basic values professed by this society —those which we have grouped together in the phrase, the 'spirit of the age'. But the truth is of course that from the very beginning this quantitative aspect of socialism has been inextricably fused with another aspect which is the qualitative critique of modern society and its spirit. That is to say, socialists have wanted not only more of existing goods (material and cultural) and their more equitable distribution: they have also demanded a fundamental reorientation of values. Alongside individual happiness they talked about also the worth of the human 'community' as being something more than its isolated, atomic particles, the individuals; they talked about ways of life radically opposed to the style established in capitalist society; they had a vision of a future where men would live simply, turning away from the pursuit of material wealth; they posed the ideals of selflessness, brotherliness, sacrifice, the voluntary acceptance of hardship in the service of the community and future generations, and they pitted these ideals against those of 'enlightened' individual self-interest. Instead

18

of the obsolescence of all kinds of moral or religious restrictions on the seeking of pleasure and happiness, they talked about a new kind of morality. Their values, in other words, have sprung only in part from the Enlightenment. In another and perhaps more significant part they have had an older origin, one moreover against which the Enlightenment itself—and the modern age as a whole—revolted in the first place.

It is no wonder then that socialism should appear as a highly complex system of ideas which, however, gains its unity in this fundamental contradiction. The centrifugal, nay explosive, tendencies of the values contained in socialism soon reveal themselves to the eyes of the observer, and they have of course made their presence and character felt at every turn in the history of the socialist movement. The important point for us to grasp is this: the heterogeneity of the origins of socialism, its simultaneous affirmation and denial of the spirit of the age, has no exact correspondence in the customary division of socialism into various 'kinds', such as communism, social democracy and the others. The truth is rather that the predominant contradiction is found in *each* of these varieties; none is exempt, none represents wholly either one or the other of the two main directions. Yet it is also the case that the basic contradiction is played out differently in each of the principal groups comprising socialism, as we shall attempt to show in more detail in subsequent chapters.

A few words will suffice here to indicate the main areas of tension and principal clashes within socialism to which we would like to draw the reader's attention. In the first place socialism moves, oscillates between individualism and collectivism, between the values of diversity and uniformity. It contains millennial expectations of a future perfect society, and it also displays moderation and realism, concentrating on the realization of immediate tasks. The spirit of compromise and accommodation is by no means foreign to it. It believes in the self-sufficiency of individual human reason, but it also recognizes false consciousness, calling for radical and forcible re-education. It emphasizes the importance of wealth-creation and at the same time repudiates its use. In the economic field socialists have espoused the values of organization, control, discipline, hierarchy, leadership by experts, even compulsion —they have also recognized and tried to come to terms with material incentives and the 'profit-motive'. Further, in the political arena socialists have professed adherence to humdrum democratism as well as to messianic elitism; they have advocated mass-spontaneity and tight organization, gradualism and revolution, bloodshed and pacifism, patriotism and cosmopolitanism. Sectarian exclusiveness and easy-going pragmatism are just as much the extreme conceptual limits of socialism as are on a different level the opposite tendencies of cultural avantgardism and the advocacy of popular mass-culture. Yet again, socialism has seen (and in part engendered) the birth of the modern 'intelligentsia' whose attitude and outlook have made it both the natural ally and also the severest critic and detractor of the rising industrial working class. The clashes of interest and multifaceted ideological oppositions between peasants, petty bourgeois, technocrats, bureaucrats, under- and overdeveloped nations, the different races and generations have also added their colour and character. All this and a lot more are part and parcel of socialism: what is this totality then, if not a mind-thrilling, fascinating paradox?

But now we seem to be in need of making another point. In the foregoing paragraphs an impression may have been given of our approach to socialism which it would be necessary to dispel. The assertion that socialism is 'self-contradictory' is not meant to be slighting or condemnatory. Quite the contrary: heterogeneity and internal tensions only show the maturity, success and worldwide establishment of the socialist idea and the socialist movement. Other political creeds escape this predicament and succeed in displaying a façade of coherence and unity only to the extent that they represent spent historical forces which can no longer accept the challenge of our times. Socialism does appear unsatisfactory on many counts, but it is at least there where the action is. We may judge it—if the plagiarism and frivolity are excused—to be the worst ideology we have got, except for all the others in the field. It is, in a rather obvious sense, the leading ideology of our age. If the list of haphazardly collected tensions and conflicts within socialism in the preceding paragraph has sounded very much like a characterization of modern politics in general, the resemblance is not fortuitous. The contradictions of socialism are the contradictions of the age: the uncertainties and desperate gropings of our modern consciousness, the characteristically modern search for human 'identity' and our ways of trying to understand the 'human predicament', our ever increasing scientific and technological power coupled with the growing recognition that the forces unleashed cannot always be subjected to conscious human control, the whole gamut of our political, economic and cultural life, with its extremism, its violence, its resignations and escapisms, fantasies and guilt-complexes, are all reflected—best reflected—in the mirror of socialism.

Socialism is the leading ideology of our age, in the first place, because in it we find in a richer and more balanced mixture than elsewhere the whole heritage of the past. In socialism the most important cultural, political, intellectual and ideological trends come together: socialism represents an aspiration to a future which is understood in terms of visions and prophecies enounced by thinkers belonging to all creeds, and believed in by masses of ordinary people in all countries. As it was eloquently expressed by Edward Bellamy at the end of the last century:

> To the stream of tendency setting toward the ultimate realization of a form of society which, while vastly more efficient for material prosperity, should also satisfy and not outrage the moral instincts, every sigh of poverty, every tear of pity, every human impulse, every generous enthusiasm, every true religious feeling, every act by which men have given effort to their mutual sympathy by drawing more closely together for any purpose, have contributed from the beginnings of civilization.[7]

The fact that today it would not come naturally to socialists to express themselves in similar terms, with the same kind of innocent optimism, shows not that socialism has run out of steam, but rather that it has successfully spread itself out, becoming an integral element in the fabric of our social and political institutions, even, in an ideological context, becoming a kind of subterranean orthodoxy. Some cooling of temper and some reduction in youthful starry-eyedness are always bound to accompany changes of this kind. Incidentally, the passage from Bellamy well illustrates one facet of the basic contradiction of socialism. It highlights the promethean task which socialism has set itself in endeavouring to reconcile and unite two opposed tendencies: the goal of efficiency for material production and the 'moral instincts'.

Furthermore, and in a less exalted manner, we might consider socialism to be the leading ideology today simply because it provides the bulk of intellectual material, in the form of books, historical, philosophical and scientific treatises, journals, pamphlets, slogans, catch-phrases and manifestoes, in the debate on, and the study of, ideologies in the widest political and academic circles. More has been written about socialism than about anything else. It is no doubt an exaggeration to suggest, as many people are wont to do, that the 'New Cold War' between Russia and China had overshadowed the conflict between socialism and capitalism. But in an ideological context this view does possess some plausibility: it is socialists of various persuasions who excel in the habit of earnestly and at length debating their doctrines, while the rest of the world just looks on, often giving the impression of playing only a supporting role in the theatre of ideologies.

This leads us to the last point. It is not too far-fetched to say even that socialism is the reigning paradigm of most modern political creeds —as it is sometimes ruefully admitted by anti-socialist writers. Socialism sets the style for politics and it deeply permeates other doctrines. Present-day conservatism, liberalism, nationalism, fascism, etc., as well as being conscious responses to the socialist challenge, are themselves to a considerable extent the partial adaptations of socialism and they are feeding on the socialist intellectual treasure-house—though of course the traffic of ideas is not entirely one way. Fascism, at least in one significant respect, is a terrible caricature and distortion of socialism. Nationalism, ideologically speaking, represents an arrest in the development towards that common solidarity and consciousness of the human race which socialists have wanted to achieve: it can be a bitter enemy of socialism as well as its partner. Conservatives and liberals unmistakably display in their theoretical assumptions as well as in their practical policies the influence of socialist ideas: the acceptance of social responsibility for general welfare and the eradication of poverty, and the political management of economies are only the most conspicuous examples. The only forces totally opposed and alien to socialism are human inertia, apathy, lack of imagination, the spiritless resignation and subservience to the sway of circumstances over man's life and destiny. And these forces are not to be discounted: they have never been totally beaten by any movement or any system of beliefs, however idealistic.

2 The Four Basic Tendencies of Socialism

We shall attempt in this chapter to give a more systematic outline to the tendencies which together make up socialist thought. As our departure we take the central argument which was advanced in the previous chapter: socialism will be interpreted as an amalgam of ideas representing both the spirit of our modern age at its fullest and at the same time its denial. To put it more concretely now: socialism gradually emerges in the eighteenth and nineteenth centuries as a series of responses to a rapidly changing human world. The great political movements and revolutions of the age, starting with the English Civil War and ending with the mid nineteenth-century upheavals, brought hopes of freedom, justice and prosperity. These revolutions came to be called 'bourgeois' revolutions subsequently, but at the time they were spearheading widely based popular movements: the fight for constitutionalism and against the arbitrary power of monarchs and the privileges of the aristocracy were popular causes. However, disappointment soon followed, when the consciousness of the Enlightenment and early classical liberalism collapsed into the world of the bourgeoisie. Feelings of disappointment and frustration were being combined with bewilderment and enmity felt towards a society which had done away with the anchors of status, security, objective moral values and conventions, without the realization of earlier hopes. Socialism is almost exactly coeval with classical liberalism: it is its reverse side, giving expression to the spiritual traumas and social and economic dislocations which were the effects of bourgeois-liberal victories. It became a stream at first of tiny, separate trickles, soon deepening and widening into a mighty river.

This flowing, swelling river of socialism consists of streams or currents. Changing the metaphor we might look upon these components as strains, streaks, limbs, boughs, elements, ingredients. In other connections we might well talk about the various principles, types, styles or traditions constituting socialism. In general, however, we shall prefer the term 'tendency' to denote the principal categories of our analysis. This is to emphasize the dynamic character of each component. They refer to actual ideas and beliefs, but also to potentialities, to a certain kind of aptness to move in definite directions. The four basic tendencies which we are going to describe below are all integral, all necessary to socialism. Each contains ideas which the popular mind as well as informed opinion have usually associated with socialism; together they provide a rounded picture, with light and shade evenly balanced. The four are mutually supporting and reinforcing tendencies: they are logically as well as historically, situationally connected, neatly dovetailing into one another almost like pieces of a jigsaw. Yet they are at the same time 'tendencies', that is, dynamic entities, which moreover have it in them to race in opposite directions, thus becoming, at their purest and most extreme, contradictions of one another.

The argument of this book is that the most satisfactory way in which we can hope to explain, do adequate justice to the meaning of socialism, is by grasping these basic tendencies. This means having to plunge below the surface of diverse doctrines and movements in order to find what is significant within them. The basic tendencies may not always be visible at first glance: they must then be abstracted, distilled from given doctrines and movements. The latter contain them mostly in a heterogeneous form, as compounds, mixtures of one another, being in addition combined with extraneous elements. But while on the one hand the basic tendencies are the results of analysis, thus being as it were 'smaller' than the actual doctrines of socialism, they are also something more than single 'unit-ideas'. This point, already mentioned in the previous chapter, must be afforded special emphasis. Single ideas in themselves have no body, no precise limits, no visible circumference. They have suggestive force only: they attract or repel as the case may be. This is especially true of values or ideals, like equality, freedom, justice and happiness, as we had occasion to note earlier. It is precisely on account of their tentativeness, their abstractness, their ambiguity, that values are the common—and hotly contested—property of a wide variety of ideologies. If, then, we are to endow the ideals of socialism with a reasonable degree of intelligibility, the task is to state them in a structured context. Even if one cannot talk in terms of strict logical relationships, one can note a certain kind of 'elective affinity' which exists among values and between values and institutions. There is cosy union among certain groups of ideas, while there may be disharmony when they are forced into contact with others. Values have other values as derivatives; they are also intimately connected with one or another institutional feature, whether political, social or economic; they also relate to favoured methods of change or maintenance of a status quo. In each instance what we have is a microcosm the bare structural elements of which should—ideally—reflect the character of the original subject of our analysis. In some cases this is easier to show than in others.

To turn then to our tendencies. The reader should get a fair warning here: the terms with which we are going to designate them will not always entirely correspond to general usage. This cannot be helped, since general usage is vague, imprecise and subject to variation. Here, however, the intention is to use these terms systematically. Besides, as will be clear from the sequel, there is some historical justification for the choice of our terms.

Egalitarianism is our first tendency. It is the *classical* principle of socialism. The dominant notion here of course is 'equality'. But while 'equality' has had several, and in most cases considerably diluted, meanings, here it has to be taken in its sharpest, purest, near-literal sense. Thus understood, equality culminates in a conception of 'community' which is considered to be higher than its individual members taken in isolation. Equality must lead logically to community: to be truly equal with your fellows in the community you must in the last resort stop being self-regarding, stop making comparisons between yourself and the next, stop wanting individually to excel over the others in the group. It means consciously accepting that self-transcendence is the truest form of self-realization, 'membership' of the community the highest form of distinction. Egalitarianism thus expresses the aspiration for a return to a 'public' or communal way of life. Its 'classicism' consists in its derivation by early socialists from the example of the Greek city-state, with special but by no means exclusive reference to Sparta.[1] With egalitarianism we find that the common ownership of goods becomes a total value, an end in itself: nothing should be allowed to stand between the single individual and his community. The egalitarian critique of capitalism thus concentrates on the baneful *division* this system imposes on the community, with overwhelming emphasis on the division into 'rich' and 'poor'.[2] The egalitarian sees relentless struggle between these two groups, with no quarter given or asked for. Egalitarianism is thus unremittingly militant: it demands fight, *revolution*, leading to the final victory which is the complete eradication of these evil divisons and the unification of mankind into one community. Politically egalitarianism obviously demands complete democracy, but democracy in its simple, classical, unitary sense, without enduring 'party' divisions. Yet it is also compatible with, and on occasions leads to the demand for, transitory educational dictatorship in the period preceding the development of full communal consciousness. The human qualities it elevates and values most highly are courage, devotion, fellow-feeling, singlemindedness, the conscious, voluntary acceptance of the need for selfsacrifice. Egalitarianism is undoubtedly the harshest, and perhaps the most unpalatable tendency we can encounter in socialism: at the same time, however, it is also the most heroic, most dynamic and noblest of all socialist principles.

Moralism, our next tendency, constitutes the *Christian* principle of socialism. It is 'Christian' not in the narrow sense, of course, suggesting that movements or individuals embracing it are or should be professing Christians. Moralism has been preached by agnostics and atheists. Yet moralism does derive from the values of Christianity,[3] and besides, it is the one principle of socialism which professing Christians can most easily accept without fear of self-contradiction. The chief values for moralism are social justice, peace, co-operation, brotherhood. Its critique of capitalism concentrates on the latter's inhumanity, its institutionalized *exploitation* of the people, especially those who have to sweat, toil in order to earn their livelihood. Capitalism is a fundamentally unjust system of society in that it inflicts misery and suffering on the very people who produce society's wealth.[4] It is cruel and inhuman in that it sets man against man, extolling selfishness and mutual enmity in the guise of 'free competition'. The moralist ideal— and this tendency is above all characterized by the stress it places on high 'ideals'—seeks to bring about justice by replacing enmity with mutual help, and fostering feelings of brotherly love and understanding among human beings. It tells us that instead of the insane and immoral scramble to amass more and more material wealth, we should find contentment with the amount we have at present, preferring service, the care of our fellows, to the pursuit of selfish individual ends. A deep feeling of responsibility for the welfare of others in our society should guide our actions. We should, furthermore, find positive satisfaction in *work*, in the creation of useful and pleasing objects. The political form most harmonious with moralist values is, again, democracy, perhaps tempered by mild notions of paternalism, and certainly pre-supposing a sense of moderation and responsibility on the part of individual citizens. Small communities as well as larger ones governed by a majoritarian system are fitting vehicles for the realization of the moralist ideal. Moralism, further, abhors war and is uneasy about revolution and violence of any kind (though not repudiating the 'just' use of force). It prefers, however, to implement desired changes by means of persuasion, appealing to men's feeling of compassion and brotherhood. Moralism holds human life sacred, but at the same time recognizes human nature as being imperfect, gullible, and in need of constant care and attention.

Rationalism, the third tendency we have to note, represents the principle of the *Enlightenment* in socialism. Here the chief values are individual happiness, reason, knowledge, efficiency in production, the rational, purposeful organization of human society in the interest of progress. The human race, rationalism maintains, has now grown up and at last freed itself from the age-old yokes of ignorance and superstition. We have in our possession 'science', the rational, ordered know-ledge of the laws of nature: we can progressively domesticate, mould nature so as to make it serve our own ends, and we can apply this knowledge also to human society. Since it is primarily material wealth (objects gained through the process of subjugating nature) that con-duces to our happiness, we should so organize our lives, our relation-ships as to secure the maximum technical, economic and administrative efficiency in all our social activities. The rationalist critique of capital-ism, therefore, decries most the *chaos* and *waste* involved in capitalist production, and its continued enthronement of ignorance and dark superstition. The political form that rationalism leads towards is also democracy, since this tendency too acknowledges the 'fundamental' equality of human beings and believes in the self-sufficiency of indi-vidual human reason. It believes, however, that democracy should be tempered with *meritocracy*, constant guidance by experts: scientists, technicians, intellectuals, people who are to be trusted with the promo-tion of general happiness. This tendency would also turn away from violent revolution as an irrational, wasteful, dangerous method of change, giving preference instead to rational persuasion, appealing this time not to man's fellow-feeling, but to his self-interest. Socialism, the rational organization of society, it holds to be the self-evident crowning of the values and aspirations of the Enlightenment: it needs only common sense and the right kind of education to make people accept it and work towards its realization.

Libertarianism, which could be termed the *romantic* principle of socialism, is the last one on our list of basic tendencies. It is the 'last' also in the sense of being the most extreme, most (at least in immediate appearance) disturbingly wild and radical among socialist principles, the very *reductio ad absurdum* of socialism. Its hitherto subterranean and secondary importance for socialist movements in the latter's history is to be explained by its extreme, even outlandish character, although it has its roots in the innermost recesses of the human psyche. Libertarianism, obviously, centres on the ideal of 'freedom', but again, as we have done with equality, we shall have to sharpen the meaning of freedom so as to make it intelligible and relevant to our analysis. Everybody—moralists, rationalists, egalitarians—wants 'freedom', but clearly no diluted sense of freedom will do here. Libertarianism is the demand for freedom in the sense of the total absence of restraints, external and internal. Its chief values are nature, human nature, sincerity, authenticity, individuality, variety, diversity, and happiness in the sense of the completely unfettered enjoyment of human instinctual energies. Libertarianism seeks to liberate man from rationality as well as convention: its search is for the 'real' man, for 'natural' man. It sees human beings as primarily passionate, emotional creatures, as 'animals' in a decidedly approbatory sense. It is, for that matter, no more unkind to say of libertarianism that it wants us to become *animals* than to say of egalitarianism that it considers us to be potential *angels*, while rationalism sees us as *machines* and moralism sees us as *children*. The libertarian critique of capitalism, at any rate, focuses on the latter's *oppressive* character, its systematic smothering and falsification of human desires. In the case of libertarianism it would be difficult to talk in terms of favoured 'political' arrangements, since this tendency would repudiate politics *in toto*. Anarchy, the absence of rules and organization, is what comes nearest to its ideal—though beware: libertarianism is not to be simply equated with 'anarchism'. Again, libertarianism too goes with the acceptance of equality in a 'fundamental' sense, except that it finds the ideal of equality in the last resort irrelevant, even meaningless. This is because equality, strictly considered, leads to the ideal of community, whereas libertarianism recognizes and is interested solely in the individual. Libertarianism, of course, looks upon what we have called the egalitarian tendency with abhorrence. Its preferred methods of change are inner conversion, 'seeing the light', and persuasion by means of example. Libertarianism is the gentlest, kindest, most tolerant of socialist tendencies; it is also—alas— the most unstable and unproductive.

These then are the four basic tendencies of socialism. They all express different socialist attitudes to the modern world. Socialism is opposed to capitalist society: but the degree and the kind of opposition for which it is the articulate expression can best be appreciated through the position of the various tendencies. To take the *degree* of opposition first, it is convenient to draw a distinction between extreme and moderate tendencies, between belief in 'revolution' and in 'evolution'. Of the four tendencies we have identified, clearly egalitarianism and libertarianism are the two committed to revolution. They are extreme, polar, pure, 'hard' tendencies: they stand for total opposition to capitalist society and for radical changes in human consciousness and social relationships. It is to be noted, furthermore, that their respective revolutionary stances point in diametrically opposed directions. If their purity is as it were further purified and their extremity pushed to the breaking-point, we reach, in the case of egalitarianism, something closely resembling what many political scientists call 'totalitarianism', whereas with libertarianism we come to a position of moral and conceptual nihilism.

Moralism and rationalism, on the other hand, are moderate, mixed, impure, intermediate, 'soft' tendencies. The attitudes they express are opposed to modern capitalist society only in part, and their respective stances involve the desire to reach accommodations, compromises, step-by-step, slow processes of change. They are often tinged with a degree of opportunism. Rationalism, one might say, accepts and to a great extent builds on the economic foundations of capitalism: it takes the productive techniques and even some aspects of the economic organization of capitalist society for granted, incorporating also the materialism and individualism characterizing this society. What it seeks is to develop them in an even more explicitly 'rational' direction. Moralism, in turn, latches on to the professed moral values of this society. It takes these more earnestly than they are being taken in capitalism, and it seeks to turn these values into really operative principles to be followed in daily life, instead of leaving them as mere façades. Both moralism and rationalism see the principal tasks of socialism to lie in constructive work, continuing to build on well-laid foundations; hence their opposition to radical breaks of any kind.

It will be, however, more interesting to see the light our tendencies may shed on the *kind* of opposition socialism offers to modern capitalist society. In this perspective the four basic principles are of course grouped differently. Moralism and egalitarianism are anti-liberal; they are backward-looking, retrogressive, atavistic; their ideals gain intellectual, and, what is much more important, emotional and psychological support from their ability to conjure up images of past and supposedly perfect forms of society. In the case of moralism this happens in a mild, moderate way: the elements it uses to make up its ideal society consist largely of suitably sterilized motifs from the Christian Middle Ages, with the emphasis on group and neighbourhood solidarity, simplicity of life, craftsmanship and the like. Egalitarianism is much bolder in its sweep, resurrecting the jarring, harsh, but glorious ideals of Antiquity. It cannot draw support from actual social experience contiguous with the present in the way that moralism can: elements of medieval mentality, after all, long survive in the age of capitalism. But egalitarianism on the other hand gives expression to what is perhaps the longest enduring, latent aspiration running through the entire span of our history since the fall of Antiquity and the rise of Christianity, leading to modern individualism: the elemental yearning after the complete union of man with man, the desire for the total reabsorption of the individual into the community.

Rationalism and libertarianism, in turn, express their opposition to capitalist society by outbidding its promises, and seeking further to develop its potentialities. Consequently, they are not anti-liberal, but hyper-liberal: their stance is audacious, confident, forward-looking, impatiently trying to rid society from all remaining shackles. These tendencies, of course, would rely for chief inspiration on the present, not on the past, and instead of conjuring up long-forgotten, dreamlike glories and perfection, they attempt to divine a future which has no resemblance to the past and only tenuous links even with the present. Again, in the case of rationalism the belief in reason and progress, albeit often militant, appears in a relatively moderate form. Here capitalism will be taken to account chiefly for its inability to fulfil its own promises with regard to the 'emancipation' of man and securing his freedom to pursue his own happiness. Libertarianism goes much further in that it attacks the values and conventions of modern capitalist society. Yet it is also fundamentally hyper-liberal, since the 'natural' man it seeks to find and liberate starts out from the 'individual' of capitalist society, man whose very 'nature' was to a large extent formed by influences operative in the modern age. Libertarianism thus

reveals itself as the purest manifestation, the highest apex of the spirit
of the age: its total opposition to the past is the reverse side of its
espousing the most explicitly modern, forward-looking potentialities
contained in the present.

It may now be of some interest to take another brief look, in the
light of our four basic tendencies, at the relationship of socialism to
other modern ideologies. In the previous chapter we made the somewhat polemical point that socialism is the leading ideology of our age,
hinting moreover that other ideologies are in a degree parasitic on
socialist ideas. Now while this will be maintained, we have to offer
further clarification and to round off the argument: the truth is that
ideologies are in a constant flux, and their individual character is always
determined by multiple and reciprocal influences. Our four tendencies
reveal socialism as a stream of ideas which is also inseparably linked
to other streams. In other words, the basic tendencies do not and
cannot serve the purpose of 'drawing a line' around socialism. Ideologies are alas not the kind of entities that could be adequately grasped by
lines being drawn around them: they do not stand to attention like
soldiers on parade, but are much more like loving couples embracing
in the dark. The student, therefore, as we have already suggested,
ought not to aspire to be a draughtsman; he should try to resemble
more closely the painter who operates with shades of colours. Green
and blue, red and yellow, are as 'different' from one another as anything
can be; yet it is impossible to describe—while remaining with the
notion of colour—at which precise point one turns into the other.
Socialism is also 'different' from liberalism, fascism, conservatism and
other similar creeds; yet what divides them are not lines but shades.
It is the moralist tendency which brings socialism into close contact
with certain aspects of modern conservatism: at one undefinable point
the ideals of welfare, charity, justice and brotherliness turn or shade
into the notion of paternalism, the values of a 'well-ordered' traditional community. Rationalism is the link which connects socialism
to liberalism: the former merely draws explicit conclusions from the
latter's basic premises. The egalitarian tendency makes socialism contiguous with fascism in a most dramatic way. While on the one hand
these two ideologies are as resolutely, as uncompromisingly opposed
to each other as any two things can be, at the same time they are intrinsically related. Fascism steals, as it were, from egalitarian socialism the
high ideals of service, devotion, sacrifice for the sake of the community,
and turns them, with a most startling *Gestalt*-switch, into their low

caricature, coupling them with racial exclusiveness, permanent dictatorship, and the worship of violence for its own sake. Finally libertarianism is the tendency which brings socialism into a close relationship with that curious bohemian underworld, the spiritual confraternity of artists, fanatics, lumpenproletarians, eccentrics, criminals, *déclassé* aristocrats and intellectuals, which, though never becoming a dynamic, cohesive social force, has always been important as a source of radical ideas and movements.[5] But all this is somewhat marginal to our present purposes.

The task now is to face squarely the question which must by now be most prominent in the reader's mind. What, after all, is the *use* of our basic tendencies, as described in the previous paragraphs? If, as was stated, they are merely abstractions from the actual doctrines of socialism, and if these doctrines contain them in a mixture, their explanatory value appears most doubtful. Indeed, it might be thought that we have chosen an easy way out: if something, some doctrine or movement, cannot be explained fully in terms of egalitarianism, then moralism, rationalism, etc. can be brought in to save our framework. But in fact the situation is not so simple.

In the first instance, our tendencies might reveal what appears most durable in socialism. Even a cursory acquaintance with the history of socialist thought in the last two hundred years shows us one thing, namely that many of the most strikingly modern-sounding arguments and formulations are repetitions or refinements of ideas advanced some considerable time ago. And this is true even though the wider doctrines themselves undergo changes. What is permanent in socialism is the basic tendencies; it is they and only they which provide the most explicit link between the 'forefathers' and present-day leaders, activists and ideologues. In the historical perspective our tendencies assume the shape of traditions: they are the threads from which the diverse doctrines of socialism are woven. Without these enduring threads there could be little or no continuity in ideological debate: after all, thinkers, and above all the socialist critics of modern society, must always speak in terms of an existing discussion, and must moreover endeavour at first to understand *present* problems in terms of *past* ideas. Thus contemporary socialist thinkers cannot help but build on the ideas bequeathed to them by their predecessors.

Now we come to a point of paramount importance. The four basic tendencies of socialism are to be found in all major socialist doctrines —this is the very hub of our whole argument. Their relative weight, however, varies from case to case. In other words, we find that one or another tendency assumes *predominance* over others in the case of a given country, doctrine, movement or historical period, and it is by virtue of this predominance that we can fruitfully employ our framework in an attempt at explanation. To be sure, this approach might not work very satisfactorily in the case of single socialist writers: in almost every instance it would involve doing some injustice to the complexity and subtlety of the individual thinker involved. Where the notion of predominance makes more sense, however, is in considering what is 'living', that is, historically significant, in the arguments put forward by socialist writers; what, in other words, has gone into the making of viable socialist movements. And even here, on the broader plane of movements, the predominance of one or another given tendency takes visible shape only at certain junctures in the historical development of socialism. At the present time, in the second half of the twentieth century, socialism does appear to be divisible into four major kinds, all of which can be made intelligible in terms of our four basic tendencies or traditions. This does not mean that such a division would have made equal sense at any earlier period since the emergence of socialism, and it does not, of course, enable us to make long-term predictions.

Given, however, that there are durable threads in socialist thought, some attention must also be paid to other factors, those in particular which are determined externally, and not by the enduring traditions. Even if the continuing identity of socialist thought gains an explanation by reference to the several tendencies, we have still not shed light on factors which themselves might explain predominance. Here, of course, no watertight, accurate and objective answers can be given, and furthermore, any answer would involve certain presuppositions about the nature of society and historical causation peculiar to one or another socialist doctrine. For this reason, we shall confine ourselves to a few schematic statements. Very broadly, we can identify three interrelated factors which would go a long way in explaining predominance. These are, firstly, the state of economic development in a society. Secondly, there is the factor of social composition. Thirdly, and this is often neglected by socialist writers, the factor of cultural traditions: these, in some cases (e.g. Britain) confined to single countries and in other cases to wider regions, take the form of ingrained habits of thought, psychic make-up and conditioned emotional responses. The cultural traditions of a country or region would often make for a closer resem-

blance between *different* ideologies obtaining there than between one
given ideology and its 'foreign' counterparts.

Let us consider this with reference to the present situation. Socialism
came into being as a result of dislocations following the modern bourgeois economic and political revolutions, partly endeavouring further
to develop and partly opposing the forces unleashed in this period.
Today, roughly two hundred years later, socialism has two major
alternative tasks, depending on which part of the world it finds itself in.
One of its roles is to be the *heir* to bourgeois civilization, both in the
ideological and in the political sense, the task being to take over from
and build on the achievements of developed capitalism. Here it finds
itself confronted by what is called 'advanced industrial society',
characterized by a fully developed capitalist class structure, the presence of cultural traditions favouring bourgeois civilization, and a high
degree of economic development, with full industrialization and a
reasonable standard of living for the majority. Secondly, socialism
finds itself in the role of having to do the work of capitalism in less
developed parts of the world. Here its task is to bring about desirable
changes in the economic, cultural and political fields *without* introducing particular features of capitalist development. Its role is to eradicate
poverty and cultural backwardness, and introduce modernization in
the shape of industrial production, a sense of modern nationhood as
well as individuality, and an acceptable standard of living for the whole
mass of people living in these parts.

Now it will appear pretty obvious that what we have above called
the 'spirit of the age' appears much more prominently in socialism operating in the developed part of the world than in the socialism
of underdeveloped countries. Socialism in the 'West' (Europe and
North America) is predominantly hyper-liberal: it has a background of fully-fledged, modern capitalism. In the rest of the world
socialism is predominantly anti-liberal: its background is still largely
the very world from which capitalism had itself sprung in the West.
This is the major division, from which all other important issues in
socialism seem to follow. To reiterate our main point: it is not simply
the case that socialism in the West *is* hyper-liberal and in the East anti-
liberal. Socialism is one: tendencies, even if they achieve predominance,
have always to coexist with and struggle against the other tendencies.
Now the major division into East and West can be seen to be further
reflected in the way the alternative tasks are seen by socialists. In the
developed world socialism can build on bourgeois economic and

cultural achievements, but there are still two fundamental questions to be asked: should progress be further accelerated, should socialists push at the frontiers of (economic) possibilities and (cultural) conventions? Or should they instead attempt to consolidate achievements, seeking to distribute the blessings of modern society more evenly? And in the underdeveloped world, given that the task is to bypass capitalism while achieving development, there are still the following two questions to be asked: should socialists proceed cautiously, preferring economic prosperity in the short-run, even at the expense of coming to terms with some aspects of the spirit of the age? Or should they push on relentlessly, with the vision of a society entirely different from bourgeois capitalism held clearly before their eyes?

There are the outstanding problems of socialism in our age. The four questions we have just formulated indicate four distinct departures for socialism. They are concretized in the four major divisions of socialism today, each showing the predominance of one out of the four basic tendencies. These major forms are *social democracy* in the developed countries of the West; *Marxist communism* in the Soviet Union and European communist states; socialism in *underdeveloped countries* in Asia, Africa and Latin-America, with special reference to communism in China and Cuba; and finally the '*New Left*' in advanced industrial countries. The division is by no means absolute: ideological cross-fertilization is constantly going on between all the four of these major forms, and not one of the four has more than a precarious kind of stability and identity. Yet it does make sense to present Western social democracy as being characterized predominantly by the basic tendency we have called moralism; Soviet-type Marxist communism is explicable mainly in terms of rationalism; socialism in the underdeveloped world gives the most distinct expression to the egalitarian tradition; and libertarianism characterizes what are perhaps the most interesting facets of the New Left in the West.

In the West the hyper-liberal aspect of socialism is strong, hence it is represented here in its extreme, libertarian form: the New Left is prominent in ideological innovations as well as in defining the techniques of political fight, whereas social democracy, representing the anti-liberal aspect of socialism only in its moderate, moralistic form, is on the defensive, being pushed further and further into a *modus vivendi* with the liberal-capitalist establishment. There is a running conflict between libertarianism and moralism as well as continual interchange of ideas and the occupation and reoccupation of doctrinal positions. Libertarianism, further, sunders itself into several and often conflicting sub-streams, such as spiritualism, quasi-religious other-worldliness, hedonism, the drug-cult, trendiness in fashion-styles and music, and sexual liberation. Social democracy, as well as being moralistic (emphasizing welfare and social justice), bears on itself also some features of its sister moderate tendency, rationalism, manifested in its preoccupation with scientific progress. And although these are the dominant types of socialism in the West, their relative instability and partial character are shown by the fact that egalitarianism, in the form of extremist sectarian groupings, instances of working-class militancy and outbreaks of terrorism, also makes its presence felt.

In the East, on the other hand, the anti-liberal aspect of socialism is stronger (in the absence of cultural traditions favouring Western-type economic and political development), being on the offensive. Hence here it is represented by its pure and extreme form of egalitarianism. This is the orthodoxy here, the basis for an understanding of native socialisms. The hyper-liberal aspect, hence, must fight an uphill struggle, and can make its impact only in a moderate, rationalist form. The two basic tendencies, egalitarianism and rationalism, are in a state of acute conflict (of which the Sino-Soviet opposition is only the most conspicuous manifestation), not excluding of course their mutual inter-penetration. Egalitarian socialism has, furthermore, its own internal dialectic, fluctuating between the two extreme poles of mass-participation, mobilization, direct democracy, and elitist dictatorship (of one charismatic leader or an entrenched group). Rationalist socialism, in its turn, is beset, *inter alia,* by the internal opposition between a more materialist orientation, with the emphasis on individual 'incentives' and the achievement of immediate prosperity, and a more idealistic line, stressing the importance of central planning and all-inclusive economic organization. But again, although these two are and are likely to remain the dominant forms, Eastern socialism is yet not entirely isolated from influences coming from the West: both moralism and libertarianism find precarious anchors in popular opposition movements, especially of course in situations where the struggle is with the 'weaker link' of dominant socialism, namely Marxist communism of the more heterogeneous, near-revisionistic, 'liberalizing' variety.

There is no point in going into further detail now regarding the four major forms of socialism, as we have the last four chapters of the book devoted to a separate discussion of each. Here we shall make just one or two general points of a more speculative nature which, however, appear to follow from the arguments hitherto advanced. The first thing we might emphasize is the curious fact that the four basic tendencies of socialism *all* have historical viability in them, and that so far no attempt to unify them completely and reduce them to one another has succeeded. (The so-called 'synthesis' attempted by Karl Marx is of course the most obvious example, and we shall have some remarks on this in Chapter Four.) Not only have the four tendencies their own dynamic, they also gain life through their contact, or even clash, with one another. It is not only physical nature that abhors a vacuum. The same seems to be the case in the world of socialism. As one socialist movement, over the course of its development, and being subject to—similarly changing—external economic and cultural determination, shows a shift in the predominance of one tendency in favour of another, we can see the tendency thus replaced reappearing in an otherwise contiguous socialist movement. Both Western and Eastern socialism display in their development the operation of this historical dialectic. Thus the predominance of libertarianism in the Western New Left is in a large part due to the increasing moderation and integration of social democracy—in the past, of course, social democracy too had the potentiality of developing in such a way as to include the libertarian and other streaks in its flow; as it, however, has shrunk to moralism, the libertarian opposition has had to come to the surface. In a much similar vein, the dilution of Marxism-Leninism with rationalism, accompanying economic and political development in Eastern Europe, has been a decisive factor in pushing Asian and other underdeveloped forms of socialism in a more distinctly and militantly egalitarian direction.

Finally, a word about the overall global destiny of socialism. The direction of socialist development has been outward, both geographically and ideologically. While it would be misleading to talk in terms of disintegration, the phenomenon could well be described as a kind of entropy or catalysis. However, this in itself could indicate either health or decay: it may very well be that socialism can best flourish in a particularized form. But going beyond this we must pronounce on what appear to be the two signal dangers facing socialism. On the one hand, socialism can become more and more polarized, losing touch with the leading elements of modern thought as well as the consciousness of the masses of ordinary people, and petrified in lifeless, outlandish positions. This leads to egalitarianism becoming perverted into totalitarian bureaucratic dictatorship, and libertarianism being reduced to ineffectual and nihilistic fantasies. Both these malformations have been exemplified in recent history and the former especially has received a great deal of adverse comment.

No less acute, however, is the other danger facing socialism, and this point deserves more emphasis than it has so far received. The danger we are talking about lies in a process the very opposite of polarization: it is the peril of depolarization, the powerful pressures pushing socialism more and more inward, towards the 'centre' of the liberal-capitalist establishment, and towards the eventual extinction of the socialist dream. This may sound too dramatic, but it is real enough: confirmation is given in the observable process whereby polar tendencies are being gradually crowded out in socialist movements and being replaced by more moderate principles. Egalitarianism in the East and libertarianism in the West have emerged in their present form because rationalism has come to dominate European Marxism, and social democracy has more or less succumbed to moralism. And what lies beyond the softer tendencies is, from the socialist point of view, the graveyard; in other words, complete surrender to the spirit of the age. In the case of European Marxism one faces the danger lying in the surreptitious 'restoration' of capitalism. In the West, where capitalism has held continuous power, this takes the form of 'accommodation', the progressive dilution of socialist principles.

But perhaps this will be enough by way of abstract theorizing. In the next three chapters we shall attempt to outline in summary form what appears relevant to our arguments in the actual historical development of socialism. Then we shall take up again the issues which were first introduced in the foregoing pages.

3 The Emergence of Socialism

If the exact boundaries of socialist thought cannot be determined with any degree of certainty, nor can the birth of socialism be designated as the foundation of one or another movement or the publication of one or another piece of writing. Instead of the birth of socialism, therefore, we should rather speak about a period of emergence during which time socialism gradually surfaces on the ideological horizon and assumes forms which it has more or less retained ever since. Even before this period, of course, we find earlier formulations, such as the religious communism of Gerrard Winstanley, the Diggers' leader in the English Civil War, which often provided inspiration for later generations without thereby establishing any meaningful sort of historical continuity. But the period of emergence proper lasts, roughly, from the mid-eighteenth century to the first quarter of the nineteenth. At this time we also see the crystallization of the distinct *logical modes* peculiar to egalitarianism, rationalism and moralism. In this chapter we shall briefly describe these, passing also some comment on early forms of the libertarian tendency. To begin with, we have to dispel a popular misconception about the Enlightenment, namely that it was a movement broadly united in its aims and presuppositions, being the 'party of humanity' locked in combat with forces of the past. In truth there was a deep split running through the whole of the Enlightenment, separating two divergent attitudes and interpretations of the interests of humanity. The split in the Enlightenment already prefigures the tensions and inner conflicts of socialism. In the eighteenth century it came to a head in the bitter enmity between the mainstream of the famous 'Philosophes', figures like Voltaire, Diderot, Helvetius and Holbach, on the one hand, and Jean-Jacques Rousseau on the other.

The Philosophes on the whole were preaching the values of knowledge and learning as against superstition; they were for progress and refinement as against stagnation, barbarity and primitive tastes. But in

social terms their views were moderate, cautiously liberal and individualistic, in some cases reactionary. They did not think too much of
the common people and were highly suspicious of equality as a social
ideal.[1] Rousseau's classicism, on the other hand, was both narrower
and of a more thoroughgoing kind. In direct and spectacular contrast to
the Philosophes, he struck a bold new note in his demand for equality
and popular sovereignty. Almost single-handed (though there were
other writers too, like Morelly and Mably, similar in persuasion and
influential at the time), he gave a dramatic new twist to modern thought,
by resurrecting the ancient egalitarian ideal. He criticized modern
society vehemently for its false values and oppressive character. The
cultivation of the arts and sciences, as well as the social and political
inequality dominating the civilized world, were his main targets. In
opposition to the principal values of the Philosophes, he elevated the
values of simplicity, honesty, faithfulness and virtue, adding to them
the martial qualities characterizing the inhabitants of the ancient city.
Further, Rousseau believed that human beings, although corrupted
by modern civilization, could resurrect and even enhance these qualities,
thereby gaining freedom and fulfilment, if they founded their communities along the right lines. They would, he argued, have to develop
social consciousness and give preference to the common interest over
and above their own particular interests. The whole community, in
the form of a 'general will', then ensures and guarantees the freedom
of its members, and keeps them in a wholesome state of equality. In
Rousseau's famous statement, in the social contract 'each of us puts
his person and all his power in common under the supreme direction
of the general will, and, in our corporate capacity, we receive each
member as an indivisible part of the whole.'[2] The general will is our
own personal will pertaining to our higher, social consciousness. It
is to this that we owe allegiance, and it is this higher understanding
which is entitled, in our own best interests, to 'force us to be free'.[3]
Rousseau's doctrine is harsh, no doubt, and it is not free of ambiguity.
It would, moreover, be absurd to ask whether or not he was a 'socialist'
in any arbitrarily chosen paradigmatic sense: he did not, in his major
writings at any rate, demand the 'public ownership' of anything.[4] Yet
it is undeniable that he is one of the chief modern sources, or perhaps
we should say transmitters, of the egalitarian tendency in socialism.
Traditions, however, grow slowly, being subject to the logic of events
in any great historical period.

The generation which prepared and enacted the colossal and cataclysmic French Revolution of 1789 was imbued with the ideas of equality and popular sovereignty. The Rousseauist influence, of course, was not the only one operative. However, as the revolution gained momentum, liberal ideas and their adherents were pushed aside by more militant groups. The *Enragés* and *Hébertists* in revolutionary Paris came to early ruin. But the Jacobins, under Robespierre and Saint-Just, were themselves being pushed into greater and greater militancy, culminating in the 'Terror'. Again, the Jacobins were not 'socialists', and, in J. L. Talmon's words, 'were most reluctant to yield to the view that there was an inconsistency between a rational political-ethical system and free economics. The Revolution forced upon them lessons against their own grain. There was a definite social dynamism in the idea of unlimited popular sovereignty. The poor were the vast majority of the nation, and thus entitled to dictate conditions to the small minority of the rich'.[6] There were levies, price control, clampdown on speculation. In this context the Jacobins' uncompromising stand on the 'one and indivisible republic' and Robespierre's cult of the 'Supreme Being' are also of the greatest significance: they all testify to the strong elective affinity between ideas making up the egalitarian tendency. Consistent egalitarianism leads not only to the stressing of the unity of the community, but also to the invocation of a unifying moral force: this may take the shape of a supernatural 'Supreme Being' or the shape of a suprapersonal 'history', or the idea of the 'nation' or the 'party'. In all instances, the deism or atheism of egalitarian socialism must be clearly distinguished from the atheism of thinkers who teach the primacy of individual happiness. Thus it was symbolic that the bust of the atheist Helvetius, prophet of hedonistic individualism, should have been removed from the Convention during the Jacobins' reign: it was now Rousseau's spirit gaining ascendancy over his Enlightenment rivals. The 'incorruptible' Maximilien Robespierre is not always counted among the 'fathers' of socialism; yet his position is absolutely central in the egalitarian tradition. The conflict between Rousseau and the Philosophes was repeated in the phase of Jacobinism between Robespierre and Danton, the former being austere and relentless in his upholding of a 'republic of virtue', the latter leaning to moderation and even libertarianism. As it is strikingly put in a recent biography: 'For Danton virtue was sex; for Maximilien it was terror. These attitudes were irreconcilable.' [7]

The heady (and for many, headless) days of Jacobinism were followed by the era of Thermidorean reaction, when the 'bourgeois' character of the revolution came to be consolidated. It was at this time that extreme Jacobinism, now languishing in opposition, fully emerged in a more easily recognizable socialistic shape. The deep-red 'communism' of François-Noel 'Gracchus' Babeuf and his associates in the 'Society of Equals' is beyond dispute. Yet Babeuf and his circle came from the extreme left wing of Jacobinism: their first objective was to restore militant Jacobin rule and the democratic constitution of 1793, and their indictment following the abortive insurrection of 1796 stressed the threat of Jacobin 'terror' more than it did the threat presented by the Babouvist design of a communist society. But the same logic which led from the Rousseauist understanding of virtue and freedom as pertaining to members of the community, to Jacobin militancy, austerity, and attempts violently to end the conflict between the rich and the poor, led also, speeded on by the pressure of events, to Babouvism.

It was Sylvain Maréchal, a faithful admirer of Rousseau, who wrote in his *Manifeste des Egaux*: 'For the true and living equality we will give up everything. Let the arts perish, if need be! But let us have true equality.' [8] The Babouvists were themselves in no doubt, in this also following in Rousseau's footsteps, that they were struggling against the 'spirit of the age', against other currents issuing out of the Enlightenment. Maréchal warns: 'True equality . . . will not be welcome to everyone. Selfish and ambitious people will curse us.' [9] And as Babeuf himself expressed it in his celebrated 'Defence': 'Society must be made to operate in such a way that it eradicates once and for all the desire of a man to become richer, or wiser, or more powerful than others.' [10] And: 'Nature has placed everyone under an obligation to work. None may exempt himself from work without committing an anti-social action.' [11] Babouvism has often been called 'crude' and 'primitive' and 'onesided', not least by later socialists. Yet the egalitarian logic, leading from the demand for absolute equality as members of the community, to the elimination of the opposition between rich and poor, to the community of possessions, is the simplest and internally most consistent among all socialist arguments. The rationale of the demand for common possessions was clearly stated by Philippe Buonarotti, Babeuf's close associate and historian of the movement:

> To the end that partiality should not disturb the social tranquility, it is necessary that all the productions of the land, and of industry, should be deposited in public magazines, whence they should issue, to be distributed equally to the citizens.[12]

Characteristically, the Babouvists followed Robespierre also in wanting to acknowledge publicly the Supreme Being, with institutional worship.[13] Their educational policies were austere, even ascetic. Buonarotti holds it to be 'important to the vigour and conservation of individuals, that the development of the passion of love, which is accelerated by early intercourse of the sexes, should be retarded.' [14] The youth of France, he argues, should be guarded from the corruption of 'effeminacy and love of voluptuous pleasures'. [15] And lastly, they believed in the right of an uncorrupted, revolutionary elite to dictate to a benighted, corrupted population. Babeuf says in his 'Defence':

> The people might, with apparent freedom, have adopted a radically vicious constitution. Lack of proper information might have prevented them from recognizing this. In such an eventuality it would be no crime to show the people how to improve matters.[16]

It is this last point, insurrection and dictatorship by a revolutionary elite, which is usually held most important in the Babouvist legacy. So it may have been in the case of such well-known figures as Auguste Blanqui, or Russian extremists like Tkachev and to some extent Lenin himself.[17] Yet it is important to bear in mind that the elitist argument itself follows from a rounded philosophy of man and society, a philosophy which contains many other features which are by no means as harsh and unpalatable as this one. The roots go back to classicism, to the yearning after the lost community. Babeuf was executed at the age of 37; he is the first great might-have-been in the history of socialism. At any rate, Jacobinism and Babouvism influenced not only insurrectionists like Blanqui but also gentler 'utopians' like Etienne Cabet, whose doctrine, incidentally, appears to have been the first one called 'communist'.

However, the French Revolution and its aftermath threw up other currents as well. Indeed, one ought to go back to the Enlightenment to show that the anti-Rousseauist, mainstream Enlightenment influence was also at work assisting the emergence of socialism. The cry, 'back to classical virtue', was vigorously opposed by the wish for 'uninterrupted progress towards the light'. It was this liberal mainstream of the Enlightenment, especially through the ideas of Condorcet, which provided the intellectual starting-point for another legendary 'founding father' of socialism, Henri de Saint-Simon. A nobleman turned commoner (he assumed the name 'Citoyen Bonhomme' in the

Revolution), Saint-Simon also took part in revolutionary events. It is an irony of history that he should have come from Picardy, the home of Gracchus Babeuf. And it is more than symbolic from the point of view of the later development of socialism that he should have been engaged in land and building speculation at the time of the austere reign of Robespierre. He was for a short time also imprisoned by the Jacobins, though it appears wrongly (being mistaken for a Belgian banker called Henri Simon).

Saint-Simon took the Enlightenment as his departure, but he was more far-seeing than the Philosophes. His was a more constructive kind of rationalism, wishing to continue the 'critical' work of the eighteenth century with a more 'constructive' nineteenth. He wanted the restoration of order, even hierarchy similar to that obtaining in the Middle Ages, on the basis of enlightened principles. He was resolutely against levelling or equality of the classical kind. In an early piece he warns his contemporaries: '. . . remember that the property-owners, though inferior in numbers, are more enlightened than yourselves, and that in the general interest, domination should be proportionate to enlightenment.' [18] And later he reaffirms his belief that merit should be rewarded by property—in the general interest. It is right, he argues, 'that the government should co-opt and endow with property those who are without property but distinguished by outstanding merit, in order that talent and property should not be divided.' [19]

How is merit to be measured? Saint-Simon was convinced that merit lay in *usefulness* to the community, in talent and effort which went into the production of useful goods. In perhaps what was 'conscious opposition' [20] to the values propagated by Rousseau and adapted by the Jacobins and Babouvists, Saint-Simon accepted modern civilization and its premises, based on the quest for individual happiness through the production and enjoyment of useful articles. 'Industry' and 'organization' were Saint-Simon's watchwords. He believed that instead of equality, which he held to be a destructive principle, the idea of 'industry' should be taken up with a view to achieving social cohesion in the post-revolutionary age. 'Where,' he asks, 'shall we find ideas which can provide this necessary and organic social bond? In the idea of industry; only there shall we find our safety and the end of the revolution.' [21] Writing in his pontifical style:

> Yes, sir, in my opinion, the sole aim of our thoughts and our exertions must be the kind of organization most favourable to

industry—industry understood in the widest sense, including every kind of useful activity, theoretical as well as practical, intellectual as well as manual.[22]

In Saint-Simon's thought the basic distinction is between 'industrial' forces, workers of all kinds, and idlers, parasites, whose social functions do not add to the well-being of society. In a very famous passage he contrasts the dangers to France which would accrue to her if she were to lose either her scientists, bankers, financiers, and skilled artisans, or her princes, rulers, politicians, and clergy. At one time he advocated the setting up of a 'Council of Newton', consisting of eminent scientists, to govern the world, replacing traditional aristocratic and ecclesiastical authority.

In the last years of his life, Saint-Simon added a new dimension to his thinking. While at first he believed, in typical Enlightenment fashion, that rational self-interest and secular scientific education were enough to ensure social harmony, the development of modern society and industry convinced him that this was not the case. He consciously moved away from even the relics of latent individualist premises in his thought, and came to condemn 'selfishness' in no uncertain terms. To combat this selfishness in the spirit of the age, he sought to found a new kind of religious consciousness, which he called the 'New Christianity'. This religion was 'called upon to achieve the triumph of the principles of universal morality in the struggle which is going on with the forces aiming at the individual instead of public interests'. And: 'It is called upon to link together the scientists, artists, and industrialists, and to make them the managing directors of the human race.' [23] Yet at the same time this new religion was designed to serve the worldly, immediate, material interests of human beings. And while Saint-Simon, as we could see from the passages above, was firm in his belief in meritocracy and leadership, he was also adamant that the 'managing directors' of society should so govern as to promote the well-being of the poorest and most numerous class. But this is only one thread which links Saint-Simon to the later development of socialism.

It has often been argued by historians and commentators that Saint-Simonism is not socialism, not, at least, in the case of the founder himself. Some leading disciples, of course, most importantly Bazard and Leroux, were preaching a quite unmistakable kind of socialism later; many well-known socialist slogans in common parlance today, for example the one which seeks to replace the capitalist 'exploitation of man by man' with the socialist 'exploitation of nature by men in union', originated with them. It is true, however, that Saint-Simon, quite apart from the fact of having influenced also the conservative positivist philosophy of August Comte, did not assert the need for common ownership. For him it appeared adequate to demand that production, especially finance and industry, should be rationally organized. Is this though very far from socialism? On the contrary, it leads to it, involving this time a logic quite different from the one which we have seen in the case of classical egalitarianism.

Here we might invoke the penetrating insight into the nature of socialism offered in Emile Durkheim's brilliant analysis, *Socialism and Saint-Simon*. Durkheim argues plausibly that in spite of surface appearances socialism is already contained in Saint-Simon's own doctrines. The logical progression here starts out not from the abstract demand for equality, but the (equally abstract) concern, common to the greatest Enlightenment thinkers from Diderot to Hume to Adam Smith, for individual well-being. It was the teaching of the early liberal philosophers and political economists that the production of wealth, leading to individual happiness, was central to social life, indeed that it was the most important human activity. As happiness came to mean in the Enlightenment the enjoyment of the products of human energy (with transcendental dimensions being more and more pushed out of focus), liberation meant the freeing of productive forces from the shackles of traditional 'political' control. It was, to put it in schematic terms, a movement away from the 'state' or 'politics' to 'society' or 'economics'. Now as Durkheim argues this process was not completed in the case of liberal thinkers and economists, who, although they thus elevated economic activity above everything else, still failed to integrate society along the lines suggested by the nature of economic activity itself. Production, though rational on the individual level, was still left arbitrary and unorganized on the level of the whole community. But if it is the case that the fruits of economic activity are the highest that society can achieve, then it follows that political concerns should be wholly subordinated to economic interests. In Durkheim's words: 'If economic interests do have the supremacy attributed to them, if, as a result, it is to these interests that human ends are reduced, the only good society can set itself is to organize industry in such a way as to secure the maximum production possible . . .' [24] And: 'Society cannot become industrial unless industry is socialized. This is how industrialism logically ends in socialism.' [25] Saint-Simonism is then the direct link between socialism and the mainstream of the Enlightenment.

We may note at this point that Durkheim's very definition of socialism, though partial (and 'legalistic'), is an exceptionally stimulating one. He draws an abstract distinction between 'socialism' and 'communism'. The former he sees as a thoroughly modern principle, the latter being the legacy of past ages. In his words: 'To so regulate the productive operations that they co-operate harmoniously—that is the formula of socialism. To regulate individual consumption in such a way that it is everywhere equal and everywhere moderate—that is the formula of communism.'[26] And: 'The society envisioned by communists is ascetic, while socialist society would be essentially industrial.'[27] Now this division is undoubtedly too rigid and formal to well serve explanatory purposes. But Durkheim does put an unerring finger on the conflicting tendencies of socialism, with special reference to the tension between rationalism (which he equated with socialism) on the one hand, and egalitarianism and moralism on the other. And he does recognize that the tendencies which he calls 'socialism' and 'communism' do not really operate in separation and isolation in the modern world, but that socialism, which is the 'heir' to communism of old, has succeeded in annexing, incorporating the latter.'[28]

In a way which bears some resemblance to the emergence of Saint-Simonism in France, English socialism has also had close, and on one side perhaps even more intimate, ties with the mainstream liberalism of the Enlightenment. Even more than in France, radical thought, representing and articulating the consciousness and interests of a strong, confident and ever-growing middle class, was steeped in the secularist, individualist, materialist values of the eighteenth century. It could, of course, be argued that Enlightenment liberalism itself had been the offspring of previous doctrinal foundations laid down by English thinkers, ranging from Thomas Hobbes to John Locke, and on a different level, Isaac Newton. The individualist-liberal tradition, at any rate, had the most fertile soil in England. It was natural that people like Voltaire and Saint-Simon should have been anglophiles, and Rousseau and Robespierre bitter anglophobes. The Rousseau-Jacobin-Babouvist tradition of socialism, though never absent, could never become predominant in English socialism. On the other hand, the doctrines of Helvetius and Beccaria were smoothly imported and became the radical orthodoxy, chiefly through such eminent thinkers as Jeremy Bentham and James Mill, whose 'utilitarianism' appeared to express the very *psyche* of modern England. Philosophical radical-ism, with its reductionist, individualist bias, and its emphasis on the 'happiness' of the individual as the highest value, held the centre of the stage. English socialism had to take its departure from here. Again, it is more than symbolic that just as Saint-Simon was a speculator, Robert Owen, the 'father' of English socialism, was a successful entrepreneur, a capitalist employer, an archetypal 'captain of industry', at one time closely allied with Jeremy Bentham in his New Lanark cotton mill, and himself the propagator of utilitarian-liberal ideas. Owen was, in E. P. Thompson's fitting terms, 'the *ne plus ultra* of Utilitarianism, planning society as a gigantic industrial panopticon',[29] 'one of the last of the 18th Century rationalists', 'setting out from New Lanark to claim the Chairmanship of the Board of Directors of the Industrial Revolution'.[30] Owen's celebrated early work, the *New View of Society*, has, to be sure, not a trace of anything recognizably 'socialist' in it. Yet Owen soon started to talk about the 'labour theory of value', about co-operation, and about the new spirit of community replacing the selfish individualism dominating English society.[31]

The fact is, and we have to attempt to reduce a very complex story to its bare essentials, that the very advance and early successes, econo-mic, political as well as intellectual, of the English middle class made it necessary for English socialism to develop in a less rationalistic direc-tion than was the hallmark of, among others on the continent, the Saint-Simonians. In England, though the rationalist Enlightenment background is unmistakable, socialism yet came to be chiefly domin-ated by conservative-moralistic motifs and tendencies. The surviving strong influence of nonconformism, itself historically connected with English liberalism, is of obvious significance here. Yet another key is to be found in the protracted and most momentous process transform-ing English society, inadequately referred to as the 'Industrial Revolu-tion'. A multiplicity of factors, only in part connected with the inven-tion of new productive techniques—the spinning-jenny alone did *not* produce capitalism—resulted in a series of events, the net outcome of which was modern England. These events involved economic and social dislocations on a large scale: they included the virtual dis-appearance of the English peasantry, the growth of towns, the intro-duction of new forms of economic organization, the increasing empha-sis on overseas trade and the ever more powerful urge to find resources and markets, the political pressure exerted by the rising entrepreneurial class, mainly through its intellectual spokesmen, the radical philosophers, on the ruling land-based aristocracy for a share of political power. Add to this the internal repercussions of the French Revolutionary and Napoleonic Wars, which led to the retardation of economic and social progress, and intensified conflict among groups thrown up by the longer-term changes referred to above. Last but by no means least we should here make special mention of the *urban industrial working class*: a group entirely new in history, one which, as the human reverse side to the class of entrepreneurs, traders and industrialists, experienced these changes only negatively; it suffered most from economic dislocations as well as from political repression.

From the point of view of socialism, the English constellation had a dual significance. On the one hand, although the goal of individual 'happiness' remained the chief aim and economic activity continued to be regarded as basic, productive efficiency, wealth-creation, was not seen as a distant goal which it was the historical task of *socialists* to bring about. Productive efficiency was already being achieved, wealth was there, being created all the time. The early English socialists, and Owen in particular, took the achievements of the Industrial Revolution for granted, lamenting rather the discrepancy between the immediate reality of wealth-creation and the baneful, socially disruptive form of wealth-distribution.[32] And as John Stuart Mill later observed, the lack of success which bands of Saint-Simonian 'missionaries' had in England was due to the fact that England had progressed beyond the state where socialists had to concentrate on the rationalization of production.[33] In other words—and let us bear in mind that we are not talking about the whole complex of English socialism, only about its predominant tendency—English socialism could *afford* to become relatively mellow, humane, moralistic in its preoccupations.

The other point is no less significant. The Industrial Revolution, and especially the presence of a poverty-stricken working class, meant that socialism in England had to become down-to-earth, literally, paying attention to the real problems, everyday livelihood concerns of real people, instead of indulging in well-meant and noble but nonetheless abstract fancies, like the achievement of 'true equality' or even the Saint-Simonian rationalist paradise. It is not, of course, the case that English socialism originated with the working class in contradistinction to 'continental' socialism—no socialist doctrine or movement *ever* had a purely working class origin; though it is true that, at least in the nineteenth century, the working class became the chief constituent and propagator of socialist ideas. It is not even the case that in

Socialism

England in the early days the poverty-stricken, hungry, ill-clad workers took much notice of socialism. But it is the case that socialists were compelled to notice, and to incorporate in their theories, the plight, the misery, the suffering of the working class. Thus it is not an accident but almost an historical necessity that in the most advanced country of the world socialism should have become the least apocalyptic, the least starry-eyed, the least given to concerns over abstract ideological 'purity'.

A few other points we have to note briefly in this connection. In England much more than elsewhere—because of the factors referred to above—the socialist critique of modern society as well as the socialist vision of the future grew out of the long and involved *three-cornered* struggle between the landed aristocracy, the rising middle class, and the poor. This gave a peculiar character to the ideology of English socialists, again making for the predominance of the moralist tendency over others. English socialism emerged as an amalgam of two opposed lines of ideological attack, taking its cue both from the critique advanced by the middle class against artistocratic reaction and privilege—taking up the 'weapons of the bourgeoisie' as Marx and Engels noted later—*and* from the critique articulated by defenders of the old order against bourgeois industrialism and commercialism. It is to be remembered that industrial capitalism, universal selfishness, 'mammon-worship' and the reign of 'dark, satanic mills' were first condemned by Tory romantics who hankered after the Middle Ages, in particular Southey, Coleridge and Carlyle (being succeeded by Disraeli, Ruskin and in a different way William Morris).

But interestingly, and perhaps somewhat confusingly, the modern radical attack on entrenched aristocratic power came also *directly* into English socialism. When one talks about the medievalist leanings of some English socialists, one does not refer to the situation immediately preceding and historically contiguous with the Industrial Revolution. After all, an important role in the changes ushering in the modern world in England was played by the *enclosure movement*, which helped destroy English rural peasant life and presented the landowners as the first modern oppressors. Thus agrarian reformers like Thomas Paine, William Ogilvie and Thomas Spence—on one side the immediate predecessors of English socialism—could draw on the people's 'fanatical and unreasoning hatred of the landed aristocracy'.[34] The hatred remained, being later metamorphosed into the characteristically English phenomenon of subdued hostility towards the bourgeoisie, as well as into the proverbial 'deference' which is due to the squire, not the trader or manufacturer. And one can also detect, in the long-standing preoccupation with dreams of a resurrected 'rural England', the almost childlike longing after the land, as testified to in countless socialist pamphlets, literary pieces, as well as the activities of early co-operative colonies, the surviving eerie echo of peasants who had been mercilessly chased away from the common land.[35]

What is important to note here is that the early English socialist critique of the bourgeoisie and the resentment felt against the landlord were coalesced together. Charles Hall, for example, writing in 1805, indicts the 'great lords', the owners of land, who 'induced ingenious men to employ their time in the production of works of art': it was 'in this manner' that 'manufactures were introduced', and now the rich can 'enjoy and consume himself the whole value of them . . .' [36] Hall, incidentally, must be one of the first writers who used the word 'capitalist' in a sense not far from our own. And William Thompson, an adherent to the philosophy of Owenite co-operativism, wrote in 1827: 'The feudal aristocracy and the aristocracy of wealth have coalesced; and those last admitted into the unholy coalition against the happiness of the great majority of their fellow-creatures, are frequently the most bitter enemies . . . of the Industrious Classes.' [37] This theme, attacking the bourgeoisie in terms of its ascendancy to aristocratic power and privilege, remains to this day in English socialism, owing to the simple reason that here, much more than anywhere else, the old landowning class and the new middle class have succeeded in forming a most viable and durable hegemony.

Another interesting point to note is that the immediate reality of wealth-creation and the presence of an industrial working class in England made for an economic orientation in socialist thinking. The ideological equivalent of the working class in socialism is the concept of 'labour', the human energy which creates wealth. The so-called 'labour theory of value', it is to be noted, comes from liberal sources, and it has a history from John Locke through Adam Smith to David Ricardo. The significance of it for socialism, however, can be easily mistaken. It is true that its eventual employment by Marx occurred in the context of a hard, rationalist, scientific theory, culminating in the Marxian prediction of the 'inevitable' demise of capitalism. But the point is that in the pre-Marxian era 'labour' in socialism had very heavy *moralistic* overtones. This signifies yet another kind of logic leading from the mainstream Enlightenment base to socialism. To

Socialism

strip it to its essentials: socialists saw that labourers, by the expenditure of their energy, created wealth. Yet they did not get their 'fair' reward; they were being cheated, injustice was done to them, as the early socialists, Owen, Piercy Ravenstone, Thomas Hodgskin and John Francis Bray, never ceased to argue. Now the relevant point to note is that the logic of labour, involving the notions of 'fairness' as well as 'reward', clashes with and is necessarily stopping short of the ideal of equality, again making for the relative predominance of conservative-moralism in English socialism. It is interesting to contrast the tone of Maréchal and Babeuf with that of William Thompson who in this respect certainly represented the feelings of the majority of English socialists. The fact that wealth is produced by labour, Thompson feels, 'introduces a limitation to equality'. He puts the point clearly: 'Non-production is a greater evil than inequality of distribution. Hence the necessity at all hazards, and by whatever miserable expedients, of upholding what was called security.' [38]

So far, then, we have noted the earliest appearances in modern socialism of three underlying socialist tendencies: *egalitarianism* developing from classical ideals through the logic of the conflict between rich and poor in circumstances of war; *rationalism* developing through the logic of progress and wealth-creation; and *moralism* through the logic of the fair distribution of wealth. We have yet to discuss in a summary fashion some early signs of what in the previous chapter we termed the 'libertarian' tendency. For rather obvious reasons, in this connection one cannot talk about 'movements' in the political, popular sense. The demand for unrestricted liberty, as we suggested earlier, comes last in the sequence of socialist concerns, although, in a latent and subdued form, its presence can often be detected, even in the period under consideration. Of course, libertarianism ought not to be confused with demands for 'freedom', without which, indeed, it would be impossible to imagine socialist programmes of whatever colouring. But libertarian notions proper also make their appearance, mostly in a scattered form, hidden in manuscripts or *obiter dicta*, as secondary concerns which their propagators held less important than the more immediate economic and political demands, and which only rarely reached the surface of public attention. In this connection we ought perhaps to mention the dark figure of the Marquis de Sade, languishing in a prison-asylum at the time of the French Revolution, and formulating his daring views on the variability of sexual appetites and their satisfaction. Libertarian notions entered the doctrines also of William Godwin, the most consistently utilitarian English thinker of all (who is erroneously seen sometimes as the 'father of anarchy', though his influence on anarchism was unimportant), and whose wife, Mary Wollstonecraft, was an early feminist. Robert Owen, too, scandalized a number of his contemporaries by his advanced, unconventional views on love and marriage. And we should not forget the teachings and exploits of the 'Saint-Simonian Church' either, who, under the leadership of Le père Enfantin and moving away from the more conventional socialism of Bazard (who died early), shocked Paris by their profession and practice of 'religious' promiscuity.

But perhaps we could most profitably gain a glimpse into libertarianism through a brief presentation of some relevant ideas of Charles Fourier, who at least is commonly considered another 'founding father' of socialism. For a long time, indeed, Fourier was seen by many as a fascinating maverick whose most important contributions to socialist doctrine were his critique of commerce and his strong advocacy of agricultural communities where labour would be made attractive, a source of constant joy, instead of the toil and sweat which it represents in civilization. Now these ideas of Fourier *are* definitely important, and we are glossing over them lightly only because in retrospect, from the vantage-point of the twentieth century, they appear less significant than others, notions which were sometimes hidden by Fourier from his contemporaries. It is the opinion of recent editors of Fourier's writings that it 'was as a critic of bourgeois society rather than capitalist economics that Fourier probably made his most original and enduring contribution to radical thought.' [39] As a critic, Fourier attacked bourgeois morality and the family system, and as a visionary he argued in favour of complete sexual liberation. Perhaps we may again note in passing that it is somewhat more than symbolic that Fourier at one time was involved in an anti-Jacobin uprising in Lyons, and that his libertarianism is combined with a quite unexpected kind of moderation when it comes to matters social and economic. Fourier, that is, while demanding complete freedom from crippling conventions, is quite happy to have both rich and poor people in his utopian 'phalanxes', even envisaging the investment of capital for profit. The point ought to prove something about the nature of 'socialism'.

Fourier's departure is not some ideal of a heavenly ancient city. He starts out from earth, from the given and unalterable natural 'passions' of the human being. These passions, he argues, are suppressed, continually frustrated in our civilized way of life, resulting in misery, strife and unhappiness. And of all the passions, which for Fourier includes even the natural tendency to intrigue and factiousness (the famous 'cabalist'), it is the most 'divine' passion, the passion of love, 'which keeps the divine fire burning in mortal men', which also 'fares worst in civilization'. Fourier goes on: 'It is given no other outlet than marriage. Isn't this enough to suggest that civilization is an order contrary to the designs of God?' [40] In his utopian world of 'Harmony' Fourier would therefore make sure that everyone was assured of a 'sexual minimum' besides the more pedestrian livelihood allowances, and even further, that all the diverse sexual interests or 'manias' as he calls them, from lesbianism and pederasty to exhibitionism, would enjoy the full blessings and organizational assistance of the whole community.

Now extreme ideas like these, of course, had no important immediate role to play in socialism in the early phase, not even in the relatively small, though at first thriving, Fourierist movements and 'phalanxes'. Yet it will be of interest to us to note that in so far as Fourierist socialism did make a public impact, it made it as a kind of socialism the direct opposite to the Jacobin and allied varieties. Under Victor Considérant, Fourier's most well-known disciple, the Fourierist school became, as George Lichtheim has noted, 'the synthesis of socialism and Romanticism'. It meant the adoption of attitudes to burning social and economic questions, always in the centre of attention for socialists, which were in the context highly unorthodox. In the period we are talking about (the 1840s), Lichtheim says, 'one could adhere to the heroic style of classical antiquity as the ideal expression of republican sentiment. But to Fourier and Considérant, no less than to the Saint-Simonians, this worship of classicism carried overtones of 1793—of revolutionary rhetoric, marching crowds, the guillotine, and the opening phase of a military adventure culminating in the Napoleonic empire; and it was of the essence of the new socialism that it was anti-militarist and anti-Jacobin.' [41] We thus come full circle.

Romanticism, the artistic and literary movement, while having Jean-Jacques Rousseau as one of its imputed founders (which is an interesting point to ponder, in view of what has been said about him in previous pages),[42] found its true home in Germany. It is not usually associated with the origins of German socialism. But we might as well note here that the romantic spirit, stressing nature, feeling, the need for authenticity, did make an impact on radical thought there, heavily colouring for example the 'communist' ideas of the famous philosopher, Ludwig Feuerbach. For Feuerbach, as for Fourier, it was also 'love' which was most important in human nature, and in the service of which Feuerbach embarked on his crusade to destroy the bases of 'alienation'. He found these bases in transcendental religion, a point on which Karl Marx sharply disagreed with him. Yet Marx's own departure was also from the same romantic roots, as we shall see in the following chapter.

4 The Nature of the Marxian Achievement

There can be little doubt about Karl Marx's significance for socialism: no other single thinker either before or after him has made an even faintly comparable impact on the development of socialist thought and socialist movements. His is a towering figure which casts a giant shadow over all lesser actors in the socialist drama. Marx has, it seems, an answer to everything. One can dislike or disagree with him, but one cannot fail to be impressed. Marx is perhaps the only political thinker who has been and is continuously 'relevant' to social problems of all kinds; he was not, unlike many of his contemporaries, just 'discovered' by successive generations, dug out of a half-forgotten limbo of past philosophies, but has always commanded attention; he is the only early 'father' figure of socialist thought with whom it is impossible even today to take up a patronizing attitude. Marx's significance, indeed, is something even more universal than socialism itself; his thought reaches out of socialism, fertilizing the broadest variety of intellectual and academic disciplines: his weight is felt in philosophy, economics, sociology, theology, natural science and even linguistics. For socialism itself Marx's appearance is the greatest, and perhaps the only, watershed. It was Marx who gave socialism its commanding intellectual stature. It was Marx who taught socialists to speak a different language, the idiom which helped to express the highest aspirations of his (and no less our own) age. Before Marx socialism is an upstart, an underdog in the realm of thought and in politics. After Marx it soon becomes a leading force in most fields. 'Since' Marx (taking our cue from the identical titles of two recent books)[1] socialism is a mature, fully grown part of the modern landscape.

In relation to his predecessors and to some extent his contemporaries, Marx's achievement appears indeed as a mighty, colossal 'synthesis', an imposing unification of diverse elements. The conventional way is to present Marx's thought as the synthetic combination and unification of French socialism, English political economy, and German idealist philosophy. But in fact it is more helpful to see his doctrine as the culmination of seven different trends of thought and social movements. Marx's thought, that is, draws on (1) the French revolutionary egalitarian-communist tradition; (2) the bourgeois rationalism of the Enlightenment which reached its highest point in Saint-Simonism; (3) utopian socialist visions of a radical alternative to bourgeois-capitalist civilization; (4) German idealist thought, especially Hegel's dialectical understanding of historical development; (5) the militant atheistic humanism and anti-authoritarianism of the romantically inclined 'Left Hegelian' thinkers; (6) the bourgeois science of political economy, with particular reference to the Ricardian 'labour theory of value'; and lastly (7) the rising dissatisfaction with capitalism as concretely manifested by the growth of working class political movements. Marxian thought unites all these, and, going beyond them, gives modern expression to the chiliastic, millenarian force of the Old Testament Hebrew prophets' teaching.

Coming down to earth, in terms of the four basic tendencies of socialism with which we have been operating, Marx's thought presents also a unity, albeit one which is considerably skewed in certain directions. In his thought it is the egalitarian and rationalist tendencies which rise to predominance. Marx holds fast on to the ultimate aim of 'communism', the total extinction of private property; and his pivotal doctrine of the 'class struggle' is but a more coherent, systematized expression of the classical conception of the conflict between the rich and the poor. And this egalitarianism in Marx is combined (and often overshadowed) by the rationalist belief in the inevitability of progress, the omnipotence of 'science' in human affairs (though not in the bourgeois sense of 'social science'), and the value of organization especially in the field of production. But alongside these basic motifs we find also in Marx's thought the tendencies which we have termed moralism and libertarianism. These two, it could be argued, were much more in evidence in the earlier phases of Marx's development, and became later incorporated in a suppressed form in the mature Marxian doctrines. Thus libertarianism is there as a kind of ultimate emotional justification of the critique which Marx hurls at the bourgeois system of society: Marx, at any rate to start with, is as impatient with all kinds of 'authority' and 'oppression', and as enthusiastic about the 'goodness' of man and of 'nature', as any warm-hearted, hot-headed romantic radical. And as we have argued, in the 'labour theory of value'

Marx merely takes over and adapts what is in essence the archetypal moralistic protest against the unjust, cruel exploitation of the worker in capitalism. To what extent Marx really succeeded in welding these tendencies into a coherent, viable doctrine of socialism is of course a highly difficult and debatable question, and we shall come back to this in due course.

Marx's departure is not socialism, but extreme bourgeois philosophical radicalism, a fact which is of considerable importance when it comes to appraising his later doctrines. Coming from a comfortable middle-class home, his youthful concerns were law, philosophy and religion, and he soon came under the sway of the radical critics and reinterpreters of Hegel, with Ludwig Feuerbach providing the chief influence. The so-called 'Young' or 'Left' Hegelians were mainly interested in liberating the 'human spirit' from the shackles of transcendental religion, and they gave a practical, humanistic twist to Hegel's idealist philosophical conclusions. They believed, and so did Marx, that the absolute idealism of Hegel pointed the way to the total elimination of all irrational forms of thought, and, by implication, traditional forms of authority—though this political conclusion was not always explicitly drawn from the Left Hegelian premises. In Feuerbach's striking formulation, the main thing to recognize was that empirical, natural, flesh-and-blood 'man' himself had potentially all the divine attributes which ignorant ages had assigned to a supernatural 'God'. Feuerbach preached what he considered the only true religion, namely the religion of man, the worship of human sentiments and emotions, 'love' being the chief one among them. Marx in the early 1840s fully subscribed to this promethean creed, and his fast growing political radicalism was at first deeply coloured by libertarian notions of a decidedly romantic character. In this, relatively short but important, phase of his development, his preoccupation was chiefly the critique of religion, Hegelian philosophy and certain features of modern society, while his substantive views were on the extreme left wing of liberalism.

But Marx soon struck out on a hitherto unbeaten track, starting to formulate his famous 'synthesis', when as a radical journalist he was compelled to leave his native Rhineland (which then belonged to Prussia), and moved to Paris where he was introduced to revolutionary socialist circles. Even more importantly, he read avidly—indeed, to intoxication—the writings of political economists. In the renowned *Manuscripts of 1844* we find Marx's first statement of his doctrines, presented in the form of a philosophical anthropology leading to the critique of *alienation*. This departure is synthetic in that it combines philosophical concepts and economic categories, highly abstract humanist premises and actual social problems. 'Man' Marx defined as potentially a 'species-being', one who, in contradistinction to animals, had the 'species', the whole human race, as the focus of his self-consciousness. Man also had a 'species-activity', singling him out from the rest of the natural world. This species-activity was 'labour', the creative application of human energy to inanimate nature. Labour, Marx insisted, had to be 'objectified', that is, congealed, incorporated in objects which satisfied, gave pleasure to their creators. Man, *homo laborans*, was thus connected to Nature in two ways: he came from and lived on Nature, having a material, sensuous, natural body; and his life-destiny, fulfilment, was the continuous 'humanization' of Nature in the course of labouring. We may note here briefly that with Marx this *active* conception of man, already to some extent prefigured in the writings of English socialists (J. F. Bray in particular), comes prominently to the fore, pushing out the earlier, typically eighteenth-century Enlightenment notion of man as a *passive* seeker after happiness—though the latter does not, of course, entirely disappear from Marxian doctrine or from socialism as a whole.

Marx notes, however, that in modern society man is most emphatically not a 'species-being', but quite the opposite. He labours, but gets no reward. As bourgeois political economy itself recognizes, Marx argues, modern society poses a contradition: 'Political economy starts from labour as the real soul of production; yet to labour it gives nothing, and to private property everything.' [2] The labouring human being—and in this society only the worker is a *human* being, properly so-called, since it is only he who engages in human species-activity, labour—is severed from the product of his labour, and this product, being independent of its creator, enslaves and rules over him. This is the state of affairs which Marx denotes by the terms 'alienation' and 'estrangement', adapting these concepts from Hegelian philosophy. As he puts the central point: '. . . the object which labour produces—labour's product—confronts it as something alien, as a power independent of the producer.' [3] It is important to realize that although 'alienation' has a number of aspects in Marx's early thought, its root meaning is the alienation of labour from its product, incurred through the process of the worker's selling, 'alienating', his creative energy for a wage. [4] From this basic alienation everything else follows. The

Socialism

worker is alienated from his own activity, from inanimate nature around
him, from the human species as a whole, from his fellows in society,
and also from himself in that he has a restricted, fragmented, self-
contradictory consciousness. He becomes a 'spiritually and physically
dehumanized being'.[5] 'The consciousness which man has of his
species is thus transformed by estrangement in such a way that the
species life becomes for him a means.' [6]

In this society life for the worker is unrelieved misery: poverty,
degradation to an animal state, despair and hopelessness are his lot.
He is ruled over by 'capital', his own product made independent; he
is subservient to the inhuman, abstract laws of the market, to universal
'exchange', exemplified by the domination of money, which Marx
calls 'the alienated ability of mankind'.[7] Owners of capital, landlords,
merchants, industrialists, are beneficiaries of this process, though not
its originators. They become rich and enjoy the produce of labour,
yet at the same time they are also 'alienated'. Marx regards them as
scarcely human: they merely exist on the alienated species-activity of
others. In their case alienation is more 'theoretical': it is manifested
in their individualist philosophies and religions.

Marx at this stage of his development paints a glowing picture of
'communism' as the 'positive transcendence of alienation', the goal
and solution of the 'riddle of history', 'the genuine resolution of the
conflict between man and nature and between man and man', 'between
freedom and necessity, between the individual and the species'.[8] Already
recognizably 'social' in his activities—such as production, industry
and scientific achievements—man is expected by Marx in this future
state to develop genuine species-consciousness. This will, Marx argues,
lead to the disappearance of religion, moral scruples, philosophy:
there will be only one 'science' both for man and for Nature. The
human senses will develop new functions and capabilities, and through
them man will discover new ways of understanding natural 'objects'
and thereby complete the process of 'humanizing' Nature. In communism, again, there will be no conflict among men, although they
will not cease to be distinct individual units. On the contrary, Marx
looks upon the 'relationship of man to woman' as the prototype of
human relations in communist society: it is in the relationship of the
sexes that man's essential oneness with nature actually *means* his oneness with the species; here this unity is experienced in a 'sensuous'
manner. It would, however, be impermissible to regard Marx on this
count as a kind of early 'sexual radical', a libertarian like Fourier.

Although libertarianism is strong in the early Marx, he regards sexual experience as essentially a *relationship*, and not, like Fourier, the blanket gratification of elemental human 'passions'. At any rate, Marx envisages the abolition of private property in the products of labour as the one crucial and indispensable method whereby to end alienation and establish communism.

Marx did not, however, remain long with vague philosophical theorizing. Already in the mid-1840s he was working towards his mature 'scientific' theories—those which became associated with his name by the first generations of 'Marxists'. The changes in Marx's emphasis, and the shift in his terminology (which is, of course, not complete: 'alienation' occurs also in *Capital*), left the main core of his views intact: he never moved away from 'communism' as the final goal, and he never ceased to look upon private property of 'capital' as his main foe. He found, however, that the framework of a 'science of history' would be a more appropriate vehicle in which to express his ideas. Thus we find formulated the famous 'materialist conception of history' in Marxian writings from 1845 onwards; by this time Marx had set up his life-long intellectual friendship with Friedrich Engels. The two exiles moved from France to Belgium, and then to England where they remained residents for the rest of their lives. The 'materialist conception of history' was their joint product: it bore the stamp of Marx's genius as well as Engels's more widespread, more mundane knowledge and experience. (We might as well mention here the fact, which may or may not be symbolic, that Engels too was a member of the class of capitalist owners, managing the family firm in Manchester. Marx was, and remained, a *déclassé* intellectual, for long periods living on the verge of poverty.)

The Marxian conception of history is 'materialist' only in the sense of locating the motive force of history in human material activity: in labour, production. Marx and Engels declare in a manuscript dating from 1845: '. . . we do not set out from what men say, imagine, conceive. . . . We set out from real, active men, and on the basis of their real life-process we demonstrate the development of the ideological reflexes and echoes of this life-process.'[9] The real life-process of men is the world of production, and here, in the 'base', Marx and Engels draw the further distinction between 'productive forces', by which they mean material processes, tools and their employment—technology in short—and the 'relations of production', meaning the organization of economic life, with particular reference to relations of property. The rest, political structures, social relations, juristic, philosophical and religious 'principles', belong to the 'super-structure', a sphere which, though not without significance, has only a dependent role to play in the forward-movement of history. In this manner Marx and Engels divide the whole of history into distinct epochs: Asiatic society, based on property owned by the state; slave-owning society in the Ancient World; feudal society in the Middle Ages with landed property and bonded serfs; and capitalist society, based on industry, wage-labour and the 'free' market.

A seemingly deterministic element enters into the picture in that the spring of historical change is seen by Marx to lie in the 'contradiction' between the development of productive forces and productive relations. The former develop smoothly, continuously: inventions are made, new discoveries occur (such as the discovery of America at the dawn of the modern age), technological processes are being perfected. The relations of production, however, assume more or less static forms in every epoch, and thus become obsolete in relation to productive forces. It is at this point that 'revolutions' do and must occur: it is the only way in which the superstructure can be brought into line with the base. But determinism does not go all the way, or rather it flows into, manifests itself in, conscious human action. The basic contradiction is actually experienced by men as social antagonism. In the opening words of the *Communist Manifesto*: 'The history of all hitherto existing society is the history of class struggles.'[10] It is always owners against workers, rulers against the oppressed, a rising class against one whose predominance is becoming outdated and thus is 'fettering' further progress. The point was put clearly and forcefully by Marx in 1847: 'For the oppressed class to be able to emancipate itself it is necessary that the productive powers already acquired and the existing social relations should no longer be capable of existing side by side. Of all the instruments of production, the greatest productive power is the revolutionary class itself.'[11] Classes thus consciously 'fight out' the contradictions. Thus slave-owning society was overthrown by the feudal barons, and thus the bourgeoisie successfully toppled feudalism.

At present the antagonism is between the bourgeoisie and the proletariat. Marx and Engels believed, certainly in the heady days of 1848–1849, that the proletarian revolution was in the offing. In the *Manifesto* (published for the 'Communist League', a small group of German exiles) they openly and confidently declared their aim to be violent revolution. 'The Communists disdain to conceal their views and aims. They openly declare that their ends can be attained only by the forcible overthrow of all existing social conditions.' [12] And for Marx the aim is still what it was in 1844: '... the theory of the Communists may be summed up in the single sentence: Abolition of private property.' [13] It is, however, to be noted that even in this truculent period the Marxian view was distinctly favourable—one could say 'fair'—to bourgeois civilization. 'In existing society, in industry based on individual exchange, anarchy of production, which is the source of so much misery, is at the same time the source of all progress.' [14] The *Manifesto* is almost laudatory in tone when depicting the 'wonders' brought about by capitalism, amongst them being—a point which is significant in view of later socialist developments—the fact that it 'rescued a considerable part of the population from the idiocy of rural life.' [15] However, now the bourgeoisie 'is unfit to rule because it is incompetent to assure an existence to its slave within his slavery ...' [16] Later, when Marx and Engels realized that capitalism still had some historical viability left in it, the 'revolutionary' aspects of their doctrine were played down, and hence the deterministic elements came more to predominate. By implication this meant also attributing even more positive value to modern society. In the 1850s, in his famous summary of the materialist conception of history, Marx declares: 'No social order is ever destroyed before all the productive forces for which it is sufficient have been developed ...' [17] And there is evidence that towards the end of his life (he died in 1883) Marx believed that at least in parts of Western Europe and North America the desired change could be brought about by conventional political means.[18]

Let us now take a look at Marx's crowning achievement as the founder of 'scientific socialism'. The materialist conception of history, for all its grand theoretical sweep, its appealing simplicity and potentialities as a general hypothesis applicable to the whole course of human history, was never worked out adequately by either Marx or Engels. In its general, abstract form it remained little more than a cluster of exciting hints, suggesting the outlines of a 'system' to end all systems. But in fact Marx as a self-consciously 'scientific' observer of history was interested in one particular epoch only, the epoch of capitalism, its genesis, its development and its decline. Marx was instrumental in establishing the inquiry known today as 'economic history'; it is in his detailed examination of the development of capitalism in England, in the renowned historical chapters of *Capital* where Marx analyses an astounding amount of material unearthed in long years of research in the Reading Room of the British Museum, that his fame as a scientist has its foundation. As G. D. H. Cole remarks in his *History of Socialist Thought*, here we see the materialist conception of history actually at work.[19] We might add that it is not to be seen anywhere else at work, discounting shorter pieces, like the brilliant but rather sketchy political and class analysis undertaken by Marx in the *Eighteenth Brumaire of Louis Bonaparte*. But this does not detract from the value of Marx's work.

The historical part of *Capital* is itself based upon the theoretical propositions of Marx's economic science; this latter is the cornerstone of Marxism. Marx's economic science has as its ostensible departure classical English political economy. It appears deterministic, almost mechanistic in its design: Marx claims to lay out the 'natural laws of capitalist production', to show tendencies 'working with iron necessity towards inevitable results'.[20] But in truth Marxian economics is a *dialectical* science to which positivist language is really unfitted. Marx did not cease to be an 'Hegelian' when he lost interest in philosophy; one could, indeed, argue that he became more of an Hegelian in his economic science. Lenin was one of the first among Marx's disciples to note the indebtedness of *Capital* to Hegel's *Logic*.[21] Since the publication of Marx's notebooks from the late 1850s (the famous *Grundrisse*),[22] the close relationship between Marx's economic categories and Hegel's dialectical conception, is, or at least is fast becoming, evident to all observers. Marx, that is to say, is operating here with the dialectical notion of *contradiction*: he looks upon basic economic categories, like labour, capital, value, money, production, consumption, circulation, trade, etc., as wholes which contain their own opposition, as *dynamic* entities which change their character in the course of time and contain within themselves the seeds of their own destruction. Indeed, it could be said that Marx's economic science is really the *synthesis* of philosophy and economics; in this sense it would not be entirely untrue to suggest that *Capital* represents merely the fully worked out notion of the 'alienation of labour' first adumbrated by Marx in the *1844 Manuscripts*.

Human labour applied to nature in the production of useful objects creates 'values'. These objects, however, are not merely used by human beings, but exchanged for one another. They thus have what Marx calls 'exchange-value': this is partly derived from use, but not wholly. What makes them exchangeable in terms of one another, substitutable for one another, is the labour which is embodied in them. This means that human labour is one general category, 'abstract labour', as Marx calls it, of which the various concrete forms of labour, the divergent skills, trades, crafts, are just manifestations which can be reduced to differing magnitudes or quantities. Thus it is possible to explain price differentials and price variations (i.e. differing exchange-values) by reference to the labour-time needed for the production of objects. This, in a nutshell, is the famous 'labour theory of value' which Marx adopts from classical political economy. He stresses, of course, in a way which we do not find with Adam Smith and Ricardo, that this general substitutability of various kinds of labour is the most important valid conclusion to be drawn from the principle of *equality*. He also puts special emphasis on the fact that this abstract equality of labour could come to the attention of economists only in modern society, with industry and manufacture, where the social character of labour became self-evident. Although it is the case that 'from the moment that men in any way work for one another, their labour assumes a social form',[23] this quality of labour becomes immediately important only in the capitalist production of 'commodities', i.e. objects (or services) sold as private property for profit.

How, then, if labour produces all values (with nature, of course), can we explain the capitalist employer's profit? Marx emphatically rejects the moralistic (and to him scientifically unsound) view that the labourer is 'cheated' by his employer in that he is paid 'less' than the natural price, i.e. exchange-value, of his labour. The labourer *does* receive his due price, that is, the amount which it takes to keep him alive and reproduce his kind—his 'subsistence' in other words. Marx's point is precisely that since employers as a class have a monopoly of 'nature' (resources and capital), they are able to pay labour what it is 'worth' in the market, that is, its exchange-value. However, Marx argues, labour is a special kind of commodity. What the labourer really sells for a price is his creative energy, his labour-*power*, and it is the chief characteristic of labour-power that it produces a *higher* value than the 'price' of the labourer. The capitalist's profit, then, is the *difference* between the labourer's 'worth' and the value of what his productive energy creates: it is a 'surplus'-value which the employer extracts by compelling the labourer to work *longer* than necessary to create the value needed for his survival. As Marx puts the argument succinctly:

Socialism

> ... the labour-process may continue beyond the time necessary
> to reproduce and incorporate in the product a mere equivalent
> for the value of labour-power. Instead of the six hours that are
> sufficient for the latter purpose, the process may continue for
> twelve hours. The action of labour-power, therefore, not only
> reproduces its own value, but produces value over and above it.
> This surplus-value is the difference between the value of the
> product and the value of the elements consumed in the formation
> of that product.[24]

Thus what appears a 'fair' and 'equal' exchange from the point of
view of bourgeois political economy (as well as bourgeois ethics), is,
seen from a higher vantage-point, also an unequal exchange between
living, creative labour and what is essentially its 'dead' product,
capital. In bourgeois terms the labourer appears 'free' to enter into
contracts of employment, but since he possesses *only* his labour-power,
and not nature, he is really forced into wage-slavery. Now, Marx
argues, 'capital obtains this surplus-labour without an equivalent,
and in essence it always remains forced labour—no matter how much
it may seem to result from free contractual agreement.'[25] Labour is
exploited by capital. As Marx puts it, in language reminiscent of his
earlier writings: 'Capital is dead labour, that, vampire-like, only lives
by sucking living labour, and lives the more, the more labour it
sucks.'[26]

However, this situation not only creates misery for the worker, but
contains the dynamics of its own eventual dissolution. Through ingenious though often difficult and ambiguous arguments Marx depicts the
further course of capitalist development, leading, through periodic
crises of over-production and the successive elimination of the 'free'
market by monopolies, to the demise of this economic and social
system. In particular he predicts, projecting observed tendencies, the
growing concentration of capital in fewer and fewer hands, the necessarily falling rate of capitalist profit with the increase in mechanization
(an argument which caused some headache to Marx's interpreters),
the sharpening of class divisions and the absorption of middle groups
into the two antagonistic camps of owners and propertyless labourers,
the growing misery of the labouring class (in absolute or relative
terms?—again, the point has never been resolved with certainty),
and the growth, as a result of all this, of revolutionary proletarian
'class consciousness' culminating in the overthrow of capitalism.

66

All the time, however, Marx stresses the positive historical role of capital. 'Development of the productive forces of social labour is the historical task and justification of capital. This is just the way in which it unconsciously creates the material requirements of a higher mode of production.'[27] This higher mode of production will then be performed 'by the fully developed individual, fit for a variety of labours, ready to face any change of production, and to whom the different social functions he performs, are but so many modes of giving free scope to his own natural and acquired powers.'[28] Production will, further, be performed by 'freely associated men', and 'consciously regulated by them in accordance with a settled plan'.[29] Labour, as an 'ever-lasting Nature-imposed condition of human existence',[30] will not disappear. But: 'Beyond it begins that development of human energy which is an end in itself, the true realm of freedom, which, however, can blossom forth only with this realm of necessity as its basis. The shortening of the working-day is its basic prerequisite.'[31]

So far, then, the overall and long-term vistas contained in Marx's teaching. We must now, however, note some other features of his doctrines, which, though deriving from the above and of lesser theoretical significance, received a great deal of attention from Marx's disciples, and, later on, his critics and would-be imitators. These features have a more immediately political, short-term importance. First of all, there is the famous Marxian doctrine of 'ideology'. Although he adapted a notion already in use, it was Marx who was chiefly responsible for the pejorative tag attached to 'ideology' by later generations. Ideas, as we have already noted, Marx regarded as secondary, determined by the actual, material conditions of society at any one time in history. 'It is not,' runs the renowned sentence, 'the consciousness of men that determines their existence, but their social existence that determines their consciousness.'[32] He held, further, that in societies characterized by social antagonism (this side of the proletarian revolution) the ideas held by most people are the 'ideas of the ruling class',[33] their function being to lull and mislead the oppressed into accepting class-rule. Ideology is thus 'false consciousness': a veil which falsifies, distorts the actual situation. Now Marx believed, obviously, that the labouring class would first have to be made aware of the true character of capitalist rule. But, it is interesting to note here, he thought also that this 'unveiling' of capitalism was a relatively easy process, already, as it were, occurring during his life-time. Hence the confidently hard, no-nonsense tone of the *Communist Manifesto*, asserting that to the proletarians 'law, morality, religion, are . . . so many bourgeois prejudices, behind which lurk in ambush just as many bourgeois interests.' [34] The same sentiment is repeated elsewhere, and it was left to Marx's later disciples, in particular Rosa Luxemburg, Georg Lukacs and Antonio Gramsci, to work out more fully the conceptual and political implications of 'false' and 'true' class-consciousness. As with so many other issues, Marx threw out ingenious hints without offering unambiguous explanations. (Incidentally, Marxists later started to use the term 'ideology' in a more general, value-neutral sense, applying it to all kinds of social and political doctrines, including Marxism itself. It is, of course, a similar value-neutral sense of 'ideology' with which we are operating in the present analysis of socialism.)

Another suggestion which Marx threw up without explaining what he precisely meant by it is the 'dictatorship of the proletariat'.[35] This concept, referring to the transitional period between the overthrow of capitalism and the establishment of full communism, follows logically from two tenets of Marx: firstly, that the existing 'state' serves merely bourgeois class interests and must therefore be destroyed in the revolution; and secondly, that even after the revolution it would take considerable time to build the new society.[36] Nevertheless, Marx never defined and indeed scarcely ever used the phrase in his writings, and the Babouvist-Blanquist overtones in the term 'dictatorship' were not lost on some of his followers. Marx, incidentally, used the phrases 'lower' and 'higher' stages of communism, to refer, respectively, to the actual building of the new society, and its culmination, when, in his words, 'the narrow horizon of bourgeois right' can 'be crossed in its entirety, and society' can 'inscribe on its banners: From each according to his ability, to each according to his needs!' [37] It was these two 'stages' of communism which Marxists later started to denote by the terms 'socialism' (lower) and 'communism' (higher).

Now even this very fleeting survey of Marx's major ideas should make us sufficiently aware of the weight and size of his contribution to socialism. We have, however, to recover our balance and attempt the difficult task of placing Marx in a perspective. The task is difficult because, as was hinted at the beginning, our very ideas on socialism today have been and are being fashioned largely by influences coming out of the Marxian powerhouse. However, it must be noted that while on the one hand Marx's significance may reach beyond socialism, on the other hand it has not, somehow, managed to embrace and fundamentally alter the nature of socialism itself. Marx refuted Feuerbach (and by implication all other 'philosophers') thus: 'The philosophers have only interpreted the world, in various ways; the point is to change it.' [38] Now it may (as yet) be unfair to ask Marx if he has in fact changed the world. But we are entitled to ask if he has changed socialism. Our analysis would suggest that in spite of his enormous impact, Marx did not entirely manage to achieve this task. He may have taught socialism to speak another language, but he has not taught it to speak without grammar and syntax, that is, in this context, without the basic tendencies. Socialism 'since Marx' may be very different from the early stages, but we still today correctly recognize contemporary socialism which is not to be identified with 'Marxism'. Marx erected an imposing theory of social change, exploitation, class-struggle and revolution, but his impact on socialism must still be regarded as a *practical* and *historical* question. In the light of the subsequent fate of the socialist movement, indeed, we are enabled to pass judgement on some weaknesses of the Marxian system, with particular attention to the theoretical sleight-of-hand with which Marx sought to impose unity where no unity can (in the real world of practice) prevail for long. It will be enough for our purposes to pinpoint two such areas in the Marxian doctrine.

Our first question must be: what is *precisely* 'communism' in Marx's teaching? We may agree with Marx on the 'utopian', irresponsible, fanciful character of attempts to write detailed blueprints for the society of the future. However, one ought not to be left in dark ambiguity with regard to the one fundamental feature of communism relevant to all ideological discussion: is it to be understood in egalitarian or in libertarian terms? Marx does, indeed, solve the problem, but only by putting a philosophical (i.e. verbal) veil over it. It is not difficult to describe communist man as the 'social individual', or 'species-being', and to warn against the 're-establishing of 'society' as an abstraction vis-à-vis the individual.' [39] In the early writings Marx appears to have been repelled by the ideals of Babouvist egalitarianism, which he called a 'regression to the unnatural simplicity of the poor and undemanding man.' [40] In later writings a more egalitarian tone prevails, Marx talking about a 'vast association' [41] of people, the establishment of 'industrial armies',[42] the elimination of 'bourgeois' individuality,[43] and the necessity for a 'directing authority' in production in the future.[44] The problem of the conflict between egalitarianism and libertarianism, however, is not solved by using apt phrases or by shirking definitions. And we must insist that it is a *real* problem: you *can* abolish the conflict between the 'individual' and 'society', but it makes all the world of a difference in which direction you want to proceed and which out of two possible objectives you want eventually to realize. The egalitarian objective is the successive elimination of the 'individual' in all its known forms, leading to its complete absorption by, melting into, the community. The libertarian objective leads to the elimination of 'society' as we understand it, the reduction of human relationships to the immediate, personal level: it makes society meaningless, irrelevant. Now there can, in certain circumstances, be an uneasy existential truce between these two polar tendencies, but a lasting fusion in *practice* there cannot—if the evidence of history is any guide. It is our contention that in so far as Marx's solution to this problem was merely theoretical, and in so far as Marxist movements tended later to stress the egalitarian tendency at the expense of its opposite (for valid historical reasons, of course), it led necessarily to critiques of Marxism assuming more or less pronounced libertarian forms.

The second ambiguity which Marx bequeathed to socialism could be expressed in terms of the inherent conflict between rationalism and moralism. The relevant question here to ask is: what exactly determines the movement of history *now*? As we have already hinted in the foregoing exposition, in Marx's teaching determinism and voluntarism, cool science and hot feeling, are combined. Now again, in point of theory there is no reason why these features could not be more or less satisfactorily fused together (and to be sure Marx makes a better job of it than perhaps anybody else), but their fusion, the much-vaunted Marxian 'unity of theory and praxis', breaks down at the very point where it counts most: in so-called 'revolutionary situations'. In so far as it is 'science', the rationalistic, impersonal explanation of historical dynamics, Marxism is of no real value in political struggle (it may, indeed, as some critics have suggested, exert an unintentionally conservative, passive 'wait-and-see' influence on socialists). And in so far as it is politics, the appeal of Marxism depends precisely on the *oblivion* it can pour over its scientific aspect. Its real, political influence for socialism has, in other words, depended on the retention and adoption of the very moralistic stance which Marx sought entirely to eradicate from the socialist vocabulary. The extraction of surplus-value from the worker may by Marx have been demonstrated through wholly objective, scientific, quantifiable arguments; but what counts is the moral substance infusing these arguments. As

E. H. Carr has expressed the point: 'In theory, Marx deplored as meaningless such abstract conceptions as justice and morality. In practice, he instinctively knew that every programme of revolt must, to be effective, appeal to a sense of righteous indignation.' [45] To this day, the moral concerns of socialism, the 'irrational' emotions felt at injustice, the oppression and exploitation of the labourer, have been far more important for Marxism than its own scientific tenets, being responsible for its worldly successes. And to the extent that Marxism claims to have superseded, in some mysterious way, the moral standpoint, it is forced to live in continuous conflict with itself.

The aforementioned theoretical weaknesses (to which we could add some more) reflect the actual historical plight of the movements which have derived their name and inspiration from Marx—of course, it would be meaningless to assign spurious causal priority to either internal-theoretical or external-practical factors. But going further we must also note that Marxism has never at any one time managed to take over, conquer the entire spectrum of socialism. It started as the creed of a small group of exiles, slowly spreading, influencing and eventually dominating the socialist movements in such key countries as Germany and Russia (to a lesser extent in France and Italy, even less in Spain, almost negligibly in Britain and North America). In the nineteenth century, however, it fought a bitter and by no means wholly victorious war against rival socialist movements, which, not surprisingly, appeared at the extremities: moderate social democratic movements on the 'Right' as it were, and militant anarchism and populism on the 'Left'. In our own era (post-1917 and especially post-1945) Marxism is unquestionably the leading ideological and political force in socialism in a world-wide context. Its heavy hegemony, in fact, might make us forgetful of its limitations. But its limitations *are* being made apparent before our eyes, and the slow, halting process of nibbling away at the outer perimeters of Marxism provides a fascinating spectacle. Attempts are continually being made to stretch Marx so as to accommodate new concerns and new departures, but at certain points the net breaks and the foundations themselves are subjected to criticism. Thus again on the extreme Right we observe social democracy severing even its vestigial links with Marx, while on the extreme Left Marx is indicted for his 'Victorian' limitations.

Another point to note is the way in which Marxism, corresponding to its global spread and increasing weight in the socialist movement, has reproduced within itself many of the tensions and conflicts which characterize socialism as a whole.[46] Here it is of considerable interest to observe how various polarizations of Marxism have been occasioning also the different emphases placed on the teaching of Marx in the latter's successive phases of development. Very broadly, one can talk about three phases in Marx's own development: philosophical humanism, revolutionary communism, scientific socialism. The last mentioned was Marx's immediate legacy, bequeathed to West European social democracy. With the rise of militant Marxism in Eastern Europe, the emphasis shifted back to the more obviously 'revolutionary' aspects of Marx, from, as it were, *Capital* to the *Manifesto*. Nearer our own age we see a similar shift of emphasis even farther back, from the political and class colouring of the *Manifesto* to the *Manuscripts*. Again, this is not an academic accident, but the reflection of another, equally real, conflict within Marxism: this time between established Marxism-Leninism and the (predominantly Western) 'New Left'. There is thus no 'real Marx' or 'authentic Marxism', just as there is no one single 'true' socialism. Moreover, cutting through these divisions, there has been and is continuing to be a yawning gap between theory and practice, between the simplified, vulgarized Marxism of the workers, activists, party-functionaries, and the rarefied, polished Marxism of the intellectuals. The former is without doubt a living political force today. The latter, in turn, provides a great deal of excitement, stimulation in intellectual and academic quarters. But its relevance to the practical needs of socialism, to the 'changing of the world' which after all was Marx's exclusive concern, is questionable. With the possible exception of Antonio Gramsci, it could be plausibly argued that the sophisticated theories of Marxist intellectuals, the Blochs, Lukacses, Adornos, Goldmans, Marcuses, Godeliers, Althussers, Collettis, are in the process of creating an inward-looking, self-sufficient literary *culture*, way above the heads of ordinary mortals. And this is scarcely what Marx himself seems to have intended or expected to happen.

5 Ideas in Ferment and the Parting of the Ways

Having in the previous chapter offered an exposition of the main contours of the Marxian system, our task now is to sketch in the milieu, political and ideological, in which the Marxian ideas operated. The period we are focusing on is the latter half of the nineteenth century. For socialism it is the age of maturation. The growing impact of socialist movements on the political life of the civilized world is clearly visible when we move from the holocaust of 1848–49 to the Russian Revolution of 1905. In 1848 the Parisian workers and socialist parties all but dominated the revolution, at least in its beginning stages, though on the whole '1848' was inspired more by radical-liberal and nationalist ideas. But from the 1860s onwards the march of socialism, replacing liberalism and nationalism on the left flank of European politics, is unmistakable. Its most dramatic impact was provided in the short-lived Paris Commune in 1871, creating a myth of 'workers in power' from which socialist movements have drawn inspiration ever since. In 1905 in Russia the impact of workers-on-strike, and abortive 'soviet' power, already foreshadow the momentous events of our own century. This period saw also the growth of socialist international organization. Here the most important landmarks are 1864, the foundation of the First International (which petered out in the 1870s, partly as a result of the defeat of the Paris Commune, and partly on account of the conflict between Marx and Bakunin), and the foundation of the Second International in 1889, this time based on the solidarity and co-operation of established socialist parties in Western Europe, and clearly dominated by orthodox German Marxism.

In the realm of ideas, too, this period holds a curious fascination. The first thing we must note is the spread of Marxian ideas in the whole of the socialist movement. Here one does not merely refer to self-professed 'Marxists', who, at any rate, considerably differed among themselves. One must note also the impact Marxism made on moderate social democracy as well as on left-wing anarchism and populism. No thinker and no movement was really exempt from this influence. The second thing we have to note is the extreme richness and variety of socialist doctrines: ideas are now in a state of flux, with fresh departures in all directions and with a confident air of anticipation shared by all. We meet a number of 'might have beens', socialist doctrines and leaders, whose contributions could have swayed the subsequent development of socialism. Our inescapable feeling is that the later fate of socialism was to a large extent due to historical accidents, reinforcing some trends and crowding out others. Thirdly, however, we have also to note that the present-day divisions within socialism already make their appearance in this age: the parting of the ways has its beginning in the latter half of the nineteenth century. Its first embryonic manifestation is to be found in the appearance of a 'Right' and a 'Left' in socialist movements, flanking the Marxist 'Centre', and already more or less corresponding to the geographical 'West' and 'East'. This, of course, is a rough approximation: the division of socialism into Right and Left almost always begs the question and is dependent on arbitrarily chosen criteria. Marxists and many other socialists would not readily accept that there is anything in socialism to the 'Left' of themselves. However, the criterion we are adopting here is a simple and straightforward one: the socialist attitude to the modern 'state'. Marxists here clearly occupied a centrist position: while they looked forward to the abolition of the state on the morrow of the revolution, at the same time they saw the necessity of using political, often constitutional, means to establish the dominance of the working class. Socialists to the Right were ready to work with the state without this ultimate aim. Those on the Left repudiated politics even in the short run.

On the Right, then, we encounter tendencies especially in France, Germany and England which came to be the chief sources of moralistic social democracy. In France the most important personalities were Christian socialists like Buchez and Lamennais, and above all Louis Blanc, member of the Provisional Government in the 1848 Revolution. Blanc was responsible for the solemn enactment of the 'Right to Work' by the revolutionary Government, although the 'Ateliers nationaux', set up by the same Government, were but a caricature of Blanc's highly idealistic plan to establish 'social workshops'. The experiment, at any rate, misfired, and indeed the whole of French social democracy was eclipsed (with Blanc being exiled to England) after the bloody 'June Days', followed later by the takeover of the government by Louis Bonaparte. Blanc's influence, however, proved fertile. In Germany moderate 'statist' socialism was given impetus by the political talents of Ferdinand Lassalle whom Bernard Shaw acknowledged to be the founder of modern social democracy.[1] Lassalle, whatever coherence and validity his views on socialism may have possessed, was unquestionably an outstanding political leader, and his party, the Allgemeine Deutsche Arbeiterverein (German General Workers' Association), proved a viable organization of the industrial working class. Lassalle, in his opposition to the growing power of the German bourgeoisie, went as far as seeking the alliance of conservative landowning interests in his fight for the workers' emancipation. His dallying with Bismarck was a shrewd manœuvre which might easily have had more lasting results. Lassalle, however, died tragically in a duel in 1864. If he had lived longer, German socialism might have taken a different course. As it was, his party in 1875 joined forces with the German Marxists, led by August Bebel and Wilhelm Liebknecht. But Lassallean ideas lived on, and it has been suggested that German social democracy, notwithstanding its orthodox Marxism, never shed the 'statism' bequeathed to it by Lassalle.

Lassalle was perhaps the most consistently 'Hegelian' socialist in Germany, since he took his cue not from a romantic transvaluation of the Hegelian dialectic (like Feuerbach and the young Marx), but from the mature Hegelian philosophy of the state. He accepted the state as 'the unity of individuals in a moral whole, a unity which increases a millionfold the power of those united', as 'the education and development of mankind for freedom'.[2] He condemned the liberal 'nightwatchman' conception of the state, and regarded it as the historic task of the working class to make the state into a really moral entity, so that, as he says in the famous 'Workers' Programme':

> ... the unhindered and free operation of individual powers should not merely come to fruition in the individual person, but that in addition it should be realized in a morally constituted community, in the solidarity of interests, communal feeling and the reciprocity of development.[3]

Turning away from the idea of a destructive revolution, Lassalle maintained that the principle of the working class (the 'Fourth Estate') was 'reconciliation' and 'love'. He thought, perhaps in retrospect naïvely, that political emancipation was a sufficient guaran-

75

tee of further progress towards socialism. Hence his call to the German workers was: 'Organize yourselves in a universal German workers' association for the purpose of lawful and peaceful, but at the same time untiring and relentless, agitation for the introduction of universal and direct suffrage in all German provinces.' [4]

England, though for different reasons, proved also to be a fertile soil where moralistic socialism could grow fairly rapidly. Whereas in Germany entrenched, essentially pre-liberal and pre-bourgeois, conservatism was the chief influence, in England socialists had to contend with a strong bourgeois ideological hegemony. Chartism, the democratic movement of the working class (tinged on its left flank with socialist ideas), more or less petered out completely by the 1850s. The co-operative movement, though helped along by eminent Owenites and Christian socialists, gradually lost its socialistic character. Mid-century Britain was dominated by liberalism. In this period, as John Saville says, 'there evolved in the vacuum thus created a labourist ideology among working men subordinate to the dominant ideas of the bourgeoisie, and this ideology thrust increasingly deep roots down into the soil of British society as the decades went by.' [5] Labourism, however, eventually supplied British socialism with one of its characteristic sources: the socialism of emotion, of moral sentiment. There was also a continuing preoccupation with the land and land reform: the re-awakening of socialism in the 1880s was, among other things, due to the appearance of Henry George's *Progress and Poverty* (1879), containing far-reaching, though (in the narrow sense) non-socialistic, proposals for justice through land-reform. Orthodox Marxism, as represented by H. M. Hyndman's Democratic (later Social Democratic) Federation, had on the whole little impact, but one should note the indirect influence of Marxian ideas on middle-class liberal socialism (Fabianism) and, more importantly, on militant trade unionism, especially in London and Scotland.

Fabian socialism, even more unmistakably than Owenism, was a direct offshoot of liberalism. It is, again, perhaps symbolic that the ideas of the greatest patron-saint of English liberalism, John Stuart Mill, should have led in a socialist direction (and also that Mill's step-daughter, Helen Taylor, became a supporter of Hyndman's Federation), though Fabian ideology is assuredly more than a 'gigantic footnote' [6] to Mill's *Principles of Political Economy*.[7] The main point about Fabianism is its acceptance of the framework of the liberal state, leading to the endeavour merely to extend democratic institutions into the

economic field. The Fabians saw socialism not as a new religion, as a
universal remedy for all human suffering, but merely as a new kind of
economic organization, which itself, furthermore, was warranted by
economic progress up to that time. 'The Fabian Society does not put
Socialism forward as a panacea for the ills of human society, but only
for those produced by defective organization of industry and by a
radically bad distribution of wealth.' [8] Its ethic was the outgrowth of
the rationalist liberal ethic of enlightened self-interest. In the words of
Sydney Olivier: 'Socialism is merely Individualism rationalized,
organized, clothed, and in its right mind.' [9] And, as Sidney Webb
explains, illustrating the peculiar blend of liberal rationalism and
moralistic socialism which the Fabian ideology represented, rational
self-interest must at one point mean the free acceptance of the claims
of the community: '. . . the perfect and fitting development of each
individual is not necessarily the utmost and highest cultivation of his
own personality, but the filling, in the best possible way, of his humble
function in the great social machine.' [10] The Fabians saw moral protest
at the injustice of capitalism to lie in the 'facts' themselves; hence their
firm conviction that 'social compunction' can best be roused by the
publication of 'authentic and impartial statistical tracts', by generating
'light' rather than 'heat'.[11] In this, with some justification, they accepted
Marx's *Capital* as their model—though, on the other hand, Fabian
thinkers (like Bernard Shaw) subjected Marx's economic doctrines to
heavy criticism. The Fabians' own economic theory consisted essentially in the updating of the Ricardian notion of 'rent' (stressing the
old radical bourgeois distinction between 'idlers' and those 'useful'
to society), combined with the Jevonian theory of final utility.

Fabianism seemed to fit perfectly the English middle-class tempera-
ment. Though the Fabian leaders numbered among them many a
colourful intellectual (such as Shaw, Annie Besant—secularist turned to
oriental mysticism—and H. G. Wells), their public image was of the
highly efficient public administrator, the cool and rational, though
socially motivated, civil servant, the learned 'social scientist'. The
Fabians wanted first and foremost to teach, to 'permeate' the top eche-
lons of political parties (first the Liberal Party and later the Labour
Party), rather than actively to lead, and least of all to organize the
working class—though they were interested in trade unionism and
inspired many an improvement in urban working-class living conditions. Educational and municipal reforms were their most significant
achievements.[12] They have, of course, remained ever since the 1880s

a living ideological force in the British labour movement, their members becoming cabinet ministers and authoritative spokesmen on British 'socialism'—of which we shall hear more in the next chapter. Yet at the same time their exaggerated emphasis on patient, non-emotional reformism, their belief in the 'inevitability of gradualness' (in Webb's renowned phrase), could be said to have cost them the mass-support which socialism needed, and which can only be purchased at the price of allowing one's blood to run high. G. K. Chesterton's verdict does not seem entirely misplaced, coming at the end of a perceptive analysis of Victorian writers: 'But while it [Fabianism] won the educated classes it lost the populace for ever. It dried up those springs of blood and tears out of which all revolt must come if it is to be anything but bureaucratic readjustment. We began this book with the fires of the French Revolution still burning, but burning low. Bernard Shaw was honestly in revolt in his own way: but it was Bernard Shaw who trod out the last embers of the Great Revolution.' [13]

There were, however, others at the time who did their utmost to keep the old fire burning. Apart from Marxism (of one kind or another), there was also 'ethical' socialism. The latter defies straightforward definitions. Historians usually refer here to Christian socialists like Steward Headlam, artists like Edward Carpenter, writers and leaders like Robert Blatchford, Bruce Glazier and Keir Hardie, whose highly emotional and moralistic conceptions of socialism constituted the chief influence behind the Independent Labour Party, founded in Bradford in 1893.[14] While devotion and human qualities of working-class leaders like Hardie ensured that the 'labourism' of the working class could at least find a suitable opening towards full political representation, journals like Blatchford's *Clarion* were highly successful in the popularization of socialist ideas. Blatchford was one of the best socialist writers in the journalistic idiom of all times. His *Merrie England* sold over a million copies, and the arguments it contains, expressed in a vivid stylistic form, provide even today one of the most convincing justifications to be found for socialism anywhere. The moralistic tendency here gains all but perfect articulation: Blatchford lashes out against capitalism in the name of age-old ideals of justice, health, and human brotherhood, and he calls for the restoration of agriculture to its old place of eminence, and for the socialization of industry to replace the present 'state of anarchy and barbarism'. His ideal is 'that each individual should seek his advantage in co-operation with his fellows',[15] a future state where the qualities of 'frugality and temperance' and the pursuit of 'higher pleasures' [16] predominate. He asks: 'Is it fair that he who does the least work should have the most money?' But he also declares his opposition to violent revolution, and shows realism in his understanding of future socialism, which, he says, is not 'a dream of a nation of stained-glass angels, who never say damn, who always love their neighbours better than themselves. . . .' [18] Shallow in some sense these and similar formulations might very well be, yet they capture what was and remains one of the principal living sources of socialism.

The epithet 'ethical' is sometimes also applied in the case of William Morris. Here, however, we encounter a brand of socialism significantly different in colour and dimension from the simple moralistic variety. Morris defies categorization perhaps more than any other socialist writer, and his stature and relevance are only beginning to be fully appreciated today. There is in his writings a large dose of moralism: his attachment to an idealized medieval rural way of life, expressed in his epic poems and the immortal descriptions of the utopian novel, *News From Nowhere*, stem from the Tory romanticism of Carlyle and Ruskin. But Morris has also hard Marxist features in his intellectual makeup: he believed, unlike his rival 'utopian' novelist, Bellamy, that socialism (he often used the stronger term 'communism') would come about as a result of violent revolution following a period of bitter struggle between the capitalist state and the working class. And although he dissociated himself in principle from anarchism, in his Socialist League he worked with anarchists and in opposition to Hyndman's orthodox Marxist Federation, sharing the anarchists' revulsion from 'politics'.[19] Of course, with Morris and the socialism of the Socialist League (which later came to be entirely dominated by anarchism), we are moving from 'Right' to 'Left' in terms of the schema adopted at the beginning of this chapter.

But Marxist though he was, Morris did not become 'Morris' simply on account of his Marxism. His interest in retrospect seems to lie chiefly in his attempts to fill the gaps left by orthodox Marxism, in his emphasis on art and on the *quality* of life in capitalism and future communism, in the attention he focused on the crippling effects of bourgeois morality on the human personality. In his frank and lucid pronouncements we find libertarian views of a markedly advanced and un-Victorian character, showing, among other things, the inherent tension between libertarianism and egalitarianism (which Morris did not, however, appear to appreciate). For example, Morris declares:

79

> ... my ideal of the Society of the future is first of all the freedom
> and cultivation of the individual will, which civilization ignores,
> or even denies the existence of; the shaking off the slavish depen-
> dence, not on other men, but on artificial systems made to save
> men manly trouble and responsibility: and in order that this will
> may be vigorous in us, I demand a free and unfettered animal
> life for man first of all: I demand the utter extinction of all
> asceticism. If we feel the least degradation in being amorous, or
> merry, or hungry, or sleepy, we are so far bad animals, and
> therefore miserable men.[20]

There is, to be sure, enough in this passage to make us want to ask
awkward questions (for example, how to reconcile 'manly trouble'
with 'unfettered animal life'). The point to note, however, is that
Morris elsewhere goes very near to articulating an almost perfect
egalitarian ethic, recognizing the need for 'authority' as a 'common
bond' among men in future society, a 'social conscience', and the
necessity to be able to distinguish in ourselves between a 'rascal or
two' (the unfettered animal?) and our higher self wanting to lead a
'manly and honourable' life.[21] In *Socialism: its growth and outcome*, a
book written by Morris jointly with E. Belfort Bax, an original Marxist
philosopher, we find perhaps what is the clearest statement of egalitarianism:

> As regards the future form of the moral consciousness, we may
> safely predict that it will be in a sense a return on a higher level
> to the ethics of the older world, with the difference that the
> limitation of scope to the kinship group in its narrower sense,
> which was one of the causes of the dissolution of ancient society,
> will disappear, and the identification of individual with social
> interest will be so complete that any divorce between the two
> will be inconceivable to the average man.[22]

And Bax, hard egalitarian that he was, goes as far as asserting in a
memorable piece on socialist ethics that in the future 'the perfect individual will ever be subordinate to the perfect society', adding the
speculative—and perfectly logical—conclusion that the ultimate end
is the complete absorption of the individual 'in a corporate social
consciousness'.[23] Further, indeed, one cannot go. Thus we find in
England at this time the whole spectrum of socialism represented by
groups and individual thinkers of varying stature and success: from

the lukewarm, muted rationalism of the Fabians and the moralists on the Right, orthodox Marxism in the centre, and the Socialist League, led by thinkers like Morris and Bax, on the Left. There are some further aspects of the socialist Left in England, to which we shall return below.

At this point it will be in order to say a few words about the United States. Here the relative failure of socialism to achieve more than a withered growth presents an interesting problem. In the early period, it should be remembered, the 'new world' of North America did show some definite promise of socialist development. Owenite and Fourierist communities were flourishing for a time, and later Marx and Engels, on account of America's rapid progress in industrialization and economic expansion, were also optimistic. (It is not very widely known that Marx was once considering emigrating to the United States.) However, these early hopes remained unfulfilled. The reasons for the relative failure of socialism in America are manifold and are closely intertwined with a wide variety of economic, social and cultural factors. A few outstanding points in this connection are worth some summary remarks.

Undoubtedly the most important reason is to be found in the vast economic opportunities presented by a continent rich in natural resources to a relatively sparse population of successive waves of European immigrants in search of wealth, security and independence. The ever-moving 'frontier' and behind it the promise of untapped material abundance absorbed a great deal of energy which in Europe was expended on attempts at social reorganization. Closely connected with this is the absence in America of the feudal-aristocratic social background which in Europe had so much to do with the emergence and particular character of socialism. Here the ideas of classical liberalism could have a full flowering; individualist private enterprise, untrammelled by the vestiges of a hierarchical social structure, could start with a clean slate. American society, further, provided equivalents and substitutes for the values of European socialism. Though on the one hand imbued with the spirit of 'self-help', acquisitiveness and rugged individualism, American society has also been thoroughly democratic and egalitarian in its social atmosphere, with a strong sense of community, team-spirit and voluntary co-operation particularly on the level of small localities. Again, although beset by extremely bitter social conflicts developing towards the end of the nineteenth century, America has also provided for a great deal of class mobility, thus forestalling the emergence of 'two nations'. Indeed, America has been not two, but a great many nations, a plurality of ethnic and racial communities—another reason for the failure in the growth of socialist consciousness. The bulk of the white American industrial working class, though no doubt 'exploited' in the Marxist sense and jealously guarding its own material interest, could always feel superior to such pariah minorities as the native Indians, the Negro slaves and their descendants, Mexicans and Puerto Ricans, and fresh, unintegrated groups of European immigrants; some of this attitude survives today in 'blue collar' trade unionism. Then, as now, socialism in its conventional forms has found a fertile soil only with these ethnic minorities, while the majority has developed its own brand of individualist ideology, peculiar to American conservatism as well as American radicalism.

America has produced, of course, a number of notable socialist leaders and thinkers. Their impact, however, has been short-lived and negligible; their ideas, though often expressed with force and eloquence, had little originality. Henry George, America's most renowned radical thinker, was not a socialist. Edward Bellamy's state-socialist utopia fell on stony ground. Eugene Debs collected almost a million votes at the presidential election in 1920, but he was not an outstanding theorist. Daniel De Leon was highly esteemed by Lenin and he had a following in Britain as well as America; his writings and oratory, however, added little to the tenets of orthodox Marxism. Thus, in spite of the very marked 'ferment of ideas' in the United States and the proliferation of radical movements, the American contribution to the development of socialism has been mainly *negative*: American society at first provided a liberal individualist alternative to socialism, while later the United States has also assumed the global role of political and military opposition to socialist regimes and movements. In the positive sense only the modern libertarian tendency in socialism stems in part from the experience and ideological style of American society; but this topic will be discussed in our last chapter.

For now, however, let us briefly comment on the phenomenon of *anarchism* which has received so far only marginal attention. It is easy to be mistaken about the nature of anarchism. It is true that 'libertarianism' (in our technical definition of this basic tendency) is most clearly articulated in the writings of some anarchist thinkers. However, it is not the case that libertarianism characterized the anarchist *movement* as a whole, or even that it predominated in the doctrines of the most

influential anarchist writers; on the contrary, we would suggest that
in so far as anarchism represented a viable movement within socialism,
it achieved this on account of the *egalitarian* features it contained.
These practical features in anarchism stood often opposed to the
libertarian sentiments voiced by anarchist thinkers. Thus anarchism
presents a case of the disjunction of theory and practice: in thought
libertarian, in action egalitarian. But this is still not the whole truth:
perhaps the best way to grasp the issue is by noting the red thread of
contradiction running through anarchist *thought* itself, being manifested in various ways in anarchist writings. The conventional distinction between 'individualist' and 'communist' anarchism does, of
course, scant justice to the complexity of the issue.

At the root of anarchism is the essentially individualist assertion of
the moral supremacy and sovereignty of the natural individual, the
vision, as the anarchist historian George Woodcock has put it, of
'free men' who 'stand godlike and kingly, a generation of princes'.[24]
On this level, that is, anarchism is out-and-out libertarian. But on the
level of concrete social doctrines—those especially which succeeded in
influencing viable movements—anarchism focuses on opposition to the
external authority and oppressive character of the bourgeois capitalist
'state'. This practical concern, however, necessarily involves a shift
from libertarianism to egalitarianism, that is, to the acceptance of
suitably *internalized* forms of 'authority', such as self-discipline,
responsibility and solidarity with the group. Pure libertarianism we
find only in the thought of Max Stirner,[25] the logical culmination of
the radical humanism of the Left Hegelian school. Stirner's radical
egoism is only the most consistent application of the Left Hegelian
romantic critique of 'alienation', issuing in the denial of any, literally,
kind of legitimate moral authority over the hard, natural individual.
Stirner's thought, it is true, is not central to anarchism (as Marxists like
Engels and Plekhanov asserted), but neither is it entirely outside the
anarchist universe of discourse.[26] Rather it represents a polar tendency,
a notion which anarchist thinkers have found most inconvenient
openly to admit to holding, but which is nevertheless lurking behind
their arguments. This notion is, of course, libertarian individualism
being revealed as the acme of the spirit of the age: no individualism
can escape the conclusion of 'nihilistic egoism' which is openly stated
by Stirner. It is well known that Marx and Engels, in spite of the full
venom of their invective and the extraordinary length of the treatment
afforded to Stirner in the *German Ideology*, did not completely succeed

in exorcizing the ghost.[27] The trend represented by Stirner later assumed greater significance through the aristocratic libertarianism of the German philosopher Friedrich Nietzsche, who, in spite of his extremely hostile denunciation of both the moralistic and egalitarian tendencies in socialism, exercised nevertheless considerable influence on later generations of socialist thinkers.[28] Yet another kind of libertarianism, articulated chiefly in the pacifist anarchism of Leo Tolstoy, became influential later, mainly through the mediation of Eastern thinkers like Gandhi.[29]

However, as far as the mainstream of anarchism is concerned in the nineteenth century, the vacillation between opposed tendencies holds good. In the case of Pierre Joseph Proudhon, for example, the 'father of anarchy', we find radical and conservative notions side by side. It was Proudhon who introduced the term 'anarchy' in a positive, approbatory sense into modern socialist literature, declaring in his famous early work, *What is Property?*: 'Property and royalty have been crumbling to pieces ever since the world began. As man seeks justice in equality, so society seeks order in anarchy.'[30] Proudhon condemns large-scale capitalist 'property', but at the same time he affirms individual 'possession' as 'the condition of social life'.[31] He also denounces in no uncertain terms 'communism' which he sees as 'oppression and slavery',[32] while he considers 'man' to be 'social by instinct', 'every day becoming social by reflection and choice'.[33] His blueprint for the future is a society of 'liberty' and 'justice', with 'mutualism' governing human relations, based on the reinvigoration of family cohesion. His is essentially a moderate, moralistic, perhaps even mildly egalitarian doctrine, a far cry from libertarianism. Yet, particularly in the light of the later development of his ideas, Proudhon's significance for socialism is enormous: he is not merely the first genuinely working-class radical theorist with a stature, but also the first coherent advocate of working-class exclusiveness and moral supremacy over the bourgeoisie. In the First International Proudhon's followers vehemently opposed the collectivization of agriculture as a socialist policy; and they were equally adamant in demanding that the working class should be represented by its own sons, workers. Not for the last time, moralism allied itself to working-class sentiment, both opposing the 'middle-class intellectual' (and intellectually vastly superior) socialism represented by Marx.

Mikhail Bakunin, Proudhon's disciple and Marx's great adversary in the First International, is at a superficial glance the most 'libertarian' of the anarchist thinkers. His intellectual origins stemmed also from the romantic powerhouse of Left Hegelianism, but, unlike Marx, he never freed himself from hotheaded romanticism. With Bakunin, of course, one must also bear in mind the Russian populist background: in retrospect he appears perhaps more important as a precursor of Russian socialism than as an exponent of anarchism—although his ideas have lately become fashionable in Western 'libertarian socialist' circles. In Bakunin the basic contradiction of anarchism is shown chiefly in the discrepancy between his most frequently voiced libertarian opinions, and the manner in which he led and organized his various anarchist movements. But even within his thought there are numerous incoherencies. He is, for example, most emphatic and exultant on the 'joy of destruction' which he considers to be a 'creative joy'. Also, not surprisingly, he makes most of the alleged connection between the belief in a supernatural God and obedience to the state, reversing thus Voltaire's famous dictum: '. . . if God really existed, it would be necessary to abolish him.' [34] And: 'The idea of God implies the abdication of human reason and justice; it is the most decisive negation of human liberty, and necessarily ends in the enslavement of mankind, both in theory and practice.' [35] Even more significantly in our context, Bakunin repudiates Rousseau, who, as he argues, 'may be considered as the real creator of modern reaction.' [36] And it comes as no surprise that he indicts the Jacobin leader Robespierre for guillotining 'the very genius of the Revolution, Danton', and preparing the way for Napoleon.[37] Also, while showing himself a rationalist adherent of the Enlightenment, Bakunin revolts in the name of individual liberty against 'science'.[38] On the other hand, Bakunin thinks that man is social by nature, and although he rejects Marx's 'authoritarian communism', he replaces Proudhonist mutualism with 'collectivism', a more easily recognizable socialistic doctrine. But what is most important to point out here is the conspiratorial, dictatorial, *Blanquist* (i.e. Jacobin) character of Bakunin's political work in anarchism, as shown in his secret organization of the 'International Brotherhood'. Georgi Plekhanov, in the classical Marxist critique of anarchism, rightly points to the 'highly fantastic centralism' [39] contained in Bakunin, while later orthodox Marxist opponents of Lenin wryly commented on the 'spirit of Bakunin' surviving in the practice of Bolshevism.[40] The quarrel between Marx and Bakunin was not conducted on the high level of principle; yet in a sense it expresses in a more developed form the conflict which we already saw appearing in the eighteenth century.[41]

The Russian aristocrat, Peter Kropotkin, was the most eminent exponent of 'communist anarchism', and also one of the most appealing anarchist writers. His human qualities (unlike the volatile, unstable Bakunin) as well as his patient, scholarly arguments command respect. However, his doctrine furnishes also a clear instance of the basic anarchist contradiction. His 'communism', indeed, is not very different from the Marxian variety, except that Kropotkin would have nothing to do with a 'transitional' period where earnings are still determined by individual 'desert'. His arguments demolishing the halfway house of collectivist socialism are worthy of attention. But his 'anarchism', beyond the obligatory denunciation of Jacobinism, seems highly suspect: it is, one feels, entirely superfluous to his communist idea (after all, Marx also envisioned the absence of government in future communist society); in addition it appears at certain points to display features which take it disturbingly close to classical laissez-faire liberal individualism. In an inexplicably naïve fashion, for example, Kropotkin would adduce examples ostensibly showing the modern tendency towards 'anarchism' taken from the world of capitalist commerce and the exchange-market! [42] Plekhanov has no difficulty in showing that *this* kind of 'anarchism', the freedom of the entrepreneur, has nothing whatever to do with 'communism'. He is justified in calling Kropotkin's thought an uneasy marriage between communism and 'Manchester philosophy'.[43] Similarly, Kautsky was right in calling attention to the anarchists' way of escaping communism and capitalist commodity production by accepting both.[44] Neither was Hyndman entirely wrong in judging anarchism to be 'in a word individualism gone mad'.[45]

However, the anarchist thinkers' libertarian language should not lead to our mistaking the character of anarchist *practice*. On this point, Marxist writers were sometimes less than fair in their criticisms. It may, with some justice, be argued that even Bakunin's fantastic conspiracies, when they had some tangible albeit short-lived results (like the Lyons uprising in 1872), were manned by revolutionaries who acted out egalitarianism. It could also be argued that the anarchists of the 'propaganda by deed' period (coinciding with Kropotkin's ascendancy as a theorist), notwithstanding the criminal nature of their activities, were still often led by the highest egalitarian motives. Their cold acceptance of death, to be sure, can only be made intelligible in terms of the strictest egalitarian ethic. Again, America provides extreme examples: it had the 'Chicago martyrs' of egalitarian anarchism, and also, in Josiah Warren and Benjamin

Tucker, outstanding individualist anarchist writers. But of course by far the most important phenomenon here is *syndicalism,* the workers' militant trade union movement which Bertrand Russell has aptly called 'the anarchism of the market-place'.[46] Syndicalism started in France in the 1890s as organized workers were harrassed by the police, leading to their unions, the 'syndicats', being turned into quasi-political bodies, geared to waging the class struggle with the most direct means possible, in places of employment. 'Anarcho-syndicalism' attracted a fairly large following (compared to other varieties of anarchism, at any rate) especially in Latin countries, but also in England and in the United States. In the latter the 'Wobblies' (Industrial Workers of the World), a syndicalist body with Marxist egalitarian leanings, had considerable impact at the beginning of this century.

Syndicalism was anarchist in the sense that it was directed against the bourgeois state. It derived in part from Proudhonist ideas, being fed by the workers' hatred of the middle class and their suspicion of intellectuals, especially those in 'parliamentary' socialist parties. But it was also heavily influenced by Marxism, and can indeed, as a recent historian has expressed it, be judged an 'extreme interpretation of the theory of the class war itself'. [47] And syndicalism was also definitely non-libertarian in that it placed the emphasis on group-loyalty, on working-class solidarity in the present struggle; and it envisaged the future organization of society also along trade-union, i.e. group, lines. The famous *Charter of Amiens* (1906) of French syndicalism lays it down as 'the duty of every working man, whatever his opinions or political or philosophical tendencies, to belong to that most essential grouping, the union.' And it declares: 'The trade union, which is today a fighting organization, will in the future be an organization for production and distribution, and the basis of social renovation.' [48] The anarchist union leader, Fernand Pelloutier, wanted the revolution to free mankind from all authority and 'every institution which has not for its essential purpose the development of production'.[49] And Tom Mann, famous British leader of 'industrial unionism', declared: 'Universal organization must carry with it industrial solidarity, i.e. universal agreement upon the object to be attained, for otherwise the capitalists will still triumph. With solidarity on the industrial field the workers become all-powerful.' [50] Talking about the 'essence of syndicalism', Mann says: 'I look for the coming of associations of equals, working co-operatively to produce with the highest efficiency, and simultaneously to care for the physical and mental well-being of all.' [51] From the syndicalist point of view quite logically, Mann alongside many others welcomed the Bolshevik takeover in Russia in 1917, and saw in 'soviet power' the nearest approximation to the syndicalist aim. Mann himself became a founder member of the Communist Party of Great Britain. Georges Sorel, too, the famous French anarcho-syndicalist philosopher, put his hopes into Lenin and the new 'proletarian state'.

The syndicalists' political strategy: relentless fight against employers on the shopfloor, and expectation of the cataclysmic 'general strike' which would paralyse the state and lead to its collapse, did not in the long run prove viable as a weapon of socialist revolution. Yet the 'myth' of the strike (which has, of course, had a long history in the working-class movement), like the 'myth' of workers' violence (both given philosophical status in Sorel's writings),[52] exercised considerable influence on socialist thinking at the turn of the century. Hotly debated at party congresses and international gatherings, the issue of the general strike (bringing in, by implication, the concept of proletarian *class-consciousness*) helped define the increasing divergence of a revolutionary, militant Marxism growing up in Eastern Europe from its parent ideological body, the orthodox Marxist German Social-Democratic Party. Within this party, the fiery Rosa Luxemburg, of Polish-Jewish origin but completely 'international' in outlook, was the most outstanding leader of the militants. Placing her faith in the masses' latent revolutionary aspirations, she bitterly denounced the reformist character of the party leadership. Eyes were now turning increasingly towards Russia where in 1905 Tsarism received a heavy blow at the hands of organized workers. The holocaust in 1917 and the final breaking up of the Second International already found socialism deeply divided: in the West moving gradually towards moderate social democracy, in the East coming finally to accept the 'Russian' path.

It will, then, be appropriate to close this chapter by briefly illuminating the character of Russian socialism. While in the West socialism developed out of liberalism (or ultimately from the mainstream of the Enlightenment), in Russia it became essentially *populist* and hence egalitarian. The main point to grasp here is the effect of the historical *discrepancy* between social development and the influx of advanced revolutionary ideas. Modern ideas had an immediate impact on Russian intellectuals (who, as in the West, came mainly from the upper classes), but no impact whatever on the great masses who still lived in feudal conditions. The only way to induce changes, therefore, lay through extreme militancy, through desperate, fanatical revolutionism. And at the same time the rural masses' own very backwardness, their surviving communal traditions and consciousness, itself *reacted* on the revolutionary intellectuals, thereby influencing the whole movement in a classical egalitarian direction. The outcome was 'populism' in the wide sense, the belief that socialism would be achieved first in Russia, and that it would be based on the 'obshchina', the village commune.[53] The great Russian revolutionary thinkers of the mid-nineteenth century, the 'Westernizer' Alexander Herzen, the writers Chernyshevsky, Ogarev, Belinsky and others, did their share in making populism an important stream in socialism. Even Marx, towards the end of his life, became interested in the Russian village commune. Russian Marxists, though committed to the materialist conception of history (which envisaged socialism coming at the apex of bourgeois-capitalist civilization), were making strenuous attempts to square the Russian populist creed with their Western-inspired rationalism. Plekhanov and Axelrod, their most eminent representatives, did not succeed in this synthesis, their ideas later developing into 'Menshevism', the counterpart of orthodox Marxist social democracy. But populism itself also contained diverging tendencies. Lavrov, for example, believed that it was necessary first to 'educate' the masses, even though it would be a long-drawn-out process, while Bakunin expected the peasants to rise spontaneously once they received the call.

But the most important line undoubtedly was the one taken by revolutionaries who thought that the revolution in Russia needed a small, disciplined, dedicated elite, charged with the task not only of engineering the revolution, but also of maintaining its momentum afterwards, forcibly educating the masses to 'freedom'. This is, of course, *Jacobinism*, which thus found its home in the East. Here we ought to mention Sergey Nechayev, one-time associate of Bakunin, who provided the prototype of the dedicated revolutionary fighter, with both the commendable and unsavoury qualities of the 'elite' strikingly embodied in his person. In his notorious 'Catechism of the Revolutionary' Nechayev declared the need for men who had no emotions, no property, no attachments, immune from romanticism, only with a 'single cold passion for revolution'.[54] Another important figure is Peter Tkachev, a student of Marxism who was before Lenin the most important theorist of Russian Jacobinism. Tkachev drew his inspiration from Babeuf and Buonarotti, and was well acquainted with

Blanquism. In true Rousseauist egalitarian fashion, Tkachev denounced bourgeois democracy which put 'the particular interest above the general interest, the partial above the whole, egoism above altruism'.[55] He based his faith in the Russian commune on the 'brotherly solidarity of all members of the commune—in other words, the ideal which was so clearly expressed in this communist legacy of the past.' [56] And although he too looked forward to enlightenment and freedom, he considered that the task was first to create 'complete and absolute equality'.[57] necessarily involving educational dictatorship. Lenin in his Geneva exile read avidly Tkachev's *Nabat*, the journal advocating the egalitarian ideal. He himself was, of course, much more than a 'Jacobin' or a Blanquist. But it was through him that the egalitarian potentials of Marxism were most powerfully brought out into the open, and implemented in practice by the Bolsheviks in and after 1917. Their story, however, will receive our attention in Chapter Six.

6 Moralism: The Way of Western Social Democracy

Social democracy at the turn of the century occupied a central position in socialism. Yet today it constitutes its 'Right wing'. The shift to some extent can be gauged by the differing connotations of the two terms, 'social democracy' and 'democratic socialism'. The former preserves its past orthodox flavour. The latter has strong, almost exclusive, associations with the present time. The older description stressed 'social' as opposed to merely legal, political, or liberal democracy; today's term focuses on 'democratic' so as to highlight the contrast between this kind of socialism and other, supposedly 'undemocratic' varieties. However, this shift in emphasis merely shows up a deep-rooted feature of West European socialism which successive historical events only helped bring to the surface. The way of Western social democracy is essentially the natural history of socialism in European countries with advanced economic structures and social formations: historical accident has acted merely as a midwife.

To understand this development, two important factors have to be remembered. The first relates to the sociological or organizational roots of social democracy, with special reference to trade unions as the economic representative organs of the working class in capitalist society. As Karl Kautsky defined it, social democracy was born of the union of the working-class movement and the idea of socialism. The second factor relates to the widely shared assumption in the nineteenth century that the introduction of universal democratic franchise in liberal-capitalist countries (together with the spread of education) would in time secure political power for the working class and bring about the victory of socialism almost as a matter of course. There were grounds at the time for this optimism. Support for social democratic parties was growing, and the general atmosphere of peace and progress lent credence to hopes of achieving socialism through socialist constitutional majorities. Jean Jaures could confidently declare: 'The great majority of the nation can be won over to our side by propaganda and lawful action, and led to complete socialism.'[1] But in the long run the outcome was quite different. Democratic franchise became a reality. Working-class power in the state did not. Socialist consciousness lagged behind. The result was the narrowing down and dilution of Western socialism, leading to the predominance of the moralist tendency.

This development took a long time, and although there is a rationale for the emergence of moralism as the predominant feature of social democracy, at certain historical junctures it looked as though the process could take different turns. Reformism and 'revisionism' appeared, however, already in the 1890s. In France the 'Possibilists' showed readiness to work for the piecemeal establishment of socialism within the confines of the liberal-republican constitution. Alexandre Millerand, a left-wing socialist leader, accepted the post of minister of commerce in Waldeck-Rousseau's government of 'republican defence' in 1899. Jean Jaures, too, gave support to non-socialist governments. In Germany von Vollmar and the more famous Eduard Bernstein called for changes in social democratic strategy and for a thorough-going 'revision' of the most cherished doctrines of Marxism. But it was growing nationalist frenzy and the imperialist policies of the European capitalist powers, culminating in the First World War, which dealt the death-blow to the unity of socialism. In abstract terms, all prominent socialist leaders opposed war and denounced imperialism, and it was believed that the great majority of the rank and file, party members and trade unionists, were also committed to peace and 'internationalism'. In the event, however, the great mass of the people supported enthusiastically their respective states in the war effort, and the 'betrayal' of internationalism by social democratic leaders only reflected mass feeling. For the French and British it appeared reasonable to fight in the defence of Western democracy against German 'militarism', while the Germans could rationalize their stand by reference to the danger of Russian Tsarist 'imperialism'. Consistently anti-war socialists were in a tiny minority. The overthrow of the Tsarist regime in February 1917 was widely welcomed by socialists. The Bolshevik takeover in October of the same year, however, was a different matter. Lenin and his followers were resolutely against the war, and besides, their doctrines and avowed methods in taking and retaining power in Russia were repellent in the eyes of many Western socialists. Add to this the Leninists' genuine and impatient belief in an impending world-wide revolution, and we have the seeds of later jealousies, conflicts, mutual recriminations and reciprocal denials of the 'socialist' label.

The world-revolution never came. Instead, Western socialist parties were now faced with a choice which on either side involved the sacrifice of principle. Alliance with the Bolsheviks meant giving up constitutionalism; repudiation of Lenin meant drawing even nearer to non-socialist parties in the Western constitutional framework. Thus the split came, giving institutional expression to the division within socialism: militant minorities (and the majority of French socialists) set up separate 'communist' parties and joined the Bolsheviks in forming the Third International. The bulk remained suspicious and increasingly hostile. There were open clashes, too, the outstanding example being the bloody defeat of German communism by the social democratic government following the First World War. For a few years the situation of the West was volatile, but with the recovery of European capitalism the lines gradually hardened. The Communist International then came entirely to be dominated by Russian power-political interests.

In the 1930s, with Italian Fascism turning aggressive and the much more menacing appearance of Nazism in Germany, socialism in the West became infused with a sense of urgency, approaching revolutionary feeling. Social democrats were resolutely opposed to Fascism while Stalin, now firmly in control in Russia, was still thinking in terms of a sharp division of Leninist communists and a blanket capitalist front including the 'social fascists' (social democrats). But events made the formation of a broad 'popular front' of anti-fascist (socialist and bourgeois) movements imperative, leading to an ideological rapprochement between the communists and their social democratic rivals. There was no unity, but certainly an alliance and an understanding, and this lasted until after the Second World War, though marred by the experience of the Spanish Civil War (with Stalin clamping down on his enemies on the Left, the anarchists and the Trotskists), the Russian purges, and, in the years following the World War, the fate of many social democrats in Eastern Europe. As a result of the Russian victory in Europe and the occupation of East European countries by the Soviet army, fresh splits occurred in social democracy, with the militant Left again uniting with the communists. Independent social democracy, of course, thereafter ceased to exist in Eastern Europe, while in the West its anti-communist orientation came more to the surface.

In the meantime, most significantly, there had been decisive changes in the nature of Western capitalism. The big financial crisis of 1929–1932 led, *inter alia*, to the working out of new methods whereby to cope with the endemic problems of over-production and unemployment. Here mention should be made of the reformist 'New Deal' administration of F. D. Roosevelt in the United States, the 'Copernican' revolution in economic thinking engineered in the main by the theories of John Maynard Keynes in Britain, and the beginning of the social democratic 'era' in Sweden. These events provided a new focus for social democratic thinking, and from then on opposition to revolutionary militancy and Soviet communism could be more confidently underlined. The War marked the ascendancy of the British Labour Party which took over from the Germans as the leading social democratic force in Europe. The Cold War saw the final hardening of the lines. Repelled by Stalinism and encouraged by the reforms in Western capitalism, social democracy evolved the shape which is still more or less extant today. The role it has assumed is that of a 'third force', between capitalism and communism. While undoubtedly (as the communists were not slow in pointing out) this has meant 'objectively' aiding Western capitalism, social democrats concentrated mainly on the tasks of welfare and economic security in the domestic scene, and on decolonization, disarmament and the possibilities of an East-West detente in the field of international relations.

To summarize then the foregoing sketch, we can pinpoint two underlying factors which were chiefly responsible for the evolving shape of social democracy. One was the unexpected viability and even popularity of reformed capitalism in the West. The other was the widespread disillusionment with militant egalitarianism. The interrelatedness of these two factors is of course quite obvious: capitalism evolved ways of securing its survival through fear of socialist revolution, while egalitarian communism was itself pushed into rigid bureaucratism through its confinement to the East.

Let us now turn to analysis. The main point about social democracy, defining its moralism, is its tendency to equate socialism with *social justice*. Other values, too, are being professed by social democrats, but it is this which gives social democracy its distinct identity. Now the significant point about social justice is that it is not—in the context—a revolutionary ideal, but one which expresses (and strengthens) moderate aspirations; it is here that the close connection between social democracy and working-class organizations bears immediate ideological fruits. Social justice calls not for radical changes in society and in individual consciousness, but for a new *balance,* a readjustment of existing elements. In more concrete terms this means being concerned with practical, immediate, 'bread-and-butter' issues, focusing on the short term and attending more to existing, present grievances than to the purity of remote ideals. It means, that is, attending to the actual, felt needs and wishes of actual people: it is in the last resort these needs and wishes which compose the elements going into the scales of justice; socialism, whatever else it may be, must also and chiefly reflect the idea of 'fairness' held by the common people. Hence the attraction of democratic processes, hence the *majoritarianism* of social democracy. As Eduard Bernstein said, the 'goal' (socialism defined purely in ideal terms) is nothing; the 'movement' (socialism as the gradual unfolding of a new system of society, a new balance) is everything. Obviously then, present capitalist society will by social democrats be afforded a positive value, since it is assumed that it is *possible* to work for the new within the confines of the old. For Bernstein as well as other social democrats socialism thus appears as 'the legitimate heir' to liberalism; democratic constitutional processes are preferred to the 'political atavism' of such methods as the dictatorship of the proletariat.[2]

We shall return to this central issue, the majoritarianism of social democracy, below. For now, let us briefly survey a few characteristic formulations selected from more recent texts and policies: these will give us the special flavour that belongs to social democracy. We must, of course, always remember that social democracy (like socialism) is not a thing, but a *range*: those who call themselves social democrats would agree on the primacy of social justice, but little else. Many in social democratic and labour parties are indistinguishable from liberals; at the other extreme social democracy is continuous with egalitarian socialism.

One interesting feature of social democracy today is its rejection of the Marxian analysis of capitalism as a society defined by the antagonism between owners of productive means and the propertyless proletariat. The 'fresh look' advocated by many social democrats reveals that present-day Western society is no longer capitalism in the old sense: secular economic changes in the scale and organization of production, and political changes leading to the increased role of the state, have caused a diminution of the significance of ownership. The state is no longer just the 'executive committee of the ruling class', but a complex organization representing a wide spectrum of interests, including the interests of a powerful working class, the latter making its weight felt through being a large part of the electorate and through trade unions. Owners of property, shareholders in private capitalist concerns, have lost their erstwhile political influence, on account partly of selective nationalization and partly of the altered character of industrial production.[3] Now although the working class has had positive gains in this process, as witness its improved standard of living and political influence, modern society in this perspective is still not fully socialist: there is a new group, a new elite, the class of industrial and commercial 'managers' and 'technocrats' holding the reins of power. This concept of a 'managerial elite' is respectable enough: in part it derives from the elitist school of sociology, exemplified in the theories of such eminent thinkers as Pareto, Michels, Mosca, and more recently James Burnham, and in part it further develops earlier social democratic theories about the 'ultra-imperialist' tendencies of capitalism advanced by Kautsky and Hilferding. The acuteness of this analysis of Western advanced industrial society is not in doubt: without presuming to pass categorical judgment on its validity as a self-sufficient explanation, we can note that it does illuminate certain features of modern society (capitalist as well as Marxist in Eastern Europe) which orthodox Marxism has found more difficult to do.

At any rate, this new understanding of capitalism has led social democrats to the seeking of new methods whereby to implement their aims. Most significantly, there has been a decisive turn away from the institutional form of 'public ownership' or 'nationalization' as the supreme means of establishing socialism. The British Labour Party, in particular, came to accept the 'mixed economy' comprising both public and private enterprise as the optimal situation. As the left-wing social democrat, Aneurin Bevan, wrote in 1952: 'It is clear to the serious student of modern politics that a mixed economy is what most people of the West would prefer.' And: 'It is neither prudent, nor does it accord with our conception of the future, that all forms of private property should live under perpetual threat.'[4] Right-wing 'revisionists' in the Labour Party went even further, successfully arguing in the 1950s for the acceptance of a new 'Amplification of Aims' by the party which sought to make the spread of common ownership only 'substantial enough to give the community power over the commanding heights of the economy.'[5] It is interesting to note that although demands for further extension of public ownership are today (1974) again being voiced by leading labour politicians in

Britain, arguments in terms of short-term economic viability are much more prominent than 'dogmatic' assertions. This makes sense. Social justice is better served by tested arrangements than by radical experimentation. As the 'mixed economies' of advanced industrial society have historically coincided with a period of relative economic security and prosperity, social democrats have shown understandable reluctance to risk upsetting the balance. Hence the emphasis shifts away from radical changes in the economic structure of modern society to efforts of achieving multi-directional amelioration within the existing system.

The social democratic assertion that present-day industrial society, as well as being 'managerial', has absorbed some important features of the traditional socialist goal, has a large amount of credibility. Modern society works, 'delivers the goods', not only in the straight economic sense, but also in the sense of political freedom, a greater amount of social equality, and a general atmosphere of toleration. Leading political parties in advanced industrial countries, whether or not social democratic, are committed to full employment, a measure of centralized economic direction, the extension of welfare provisions, and freedom of trade union organization (including the right to strike). It is, of course, true that past efforts of social democracy in the more militant period have had a decisive share in bringing about this state of affairs. Thus it appears not entirely illogical—from the social democratic viewpoint—that the traditional goals of socialism be now expressed in terms of humanitarianism and compassion—for this is as much as the majority of the people can be presumed to accept without turning away from social democracy. The majority in these societies, many social democrats would maintain, live in prosperity: socialism for them should above all mean awareness of the plight of a minority within as well as the masses living in the underdeveloped part of the world. 'Be unselfish', 'give generously'—are the slogans. Roy Jenkins of the Labour Party, for example, has called for 'idealism' on the part of the people. 'We have to persuade men and women who are themselves reasonably well off that they have a duty to forgo some of the advantages they would otherwise enjoy for the sake of others who are much poorer than they are.' And: '. . . the gulf between majority and minority now cuts across class lines. Our only hope is to appeal to the latent idealism of all men and women of goodwill . . .'[6] Apart from this moral awareness, we find other traditional socialist goals in present-day social democracy, sometimes stressed, but often appearing

97

in a subdued or diluted form, for instance the abolition of educational privileges and the extension of industrial democracy and participation.[7]

In all this it is of special interest to note the 'liberal connection'. In their theoretical assumptions as well as their concerns and policies, social democrats closely follow in the footsteps of classical liberalism. Their understanding of democracy, for example, usually involves the admission of *permanent* clashes of interest among people. In the words of Evan Durbin, the eminent social democratic theorist, 'disagreement between individuals is of the very essence of human personality.'[8] Hence he regards the 'mutual toleration between opposing Parties'[9] as the essential feature of democracy. We find also the traditional concerns of liberalism in the political field now being espoused by social democracy. Both liberals and social democrats are great 'protesters'. In the nineteenth century it was slavery, imperialism and various 'atrocities'. Today it tends to be the arms race, great-power aggression, racialism and right-wing (fascist or military) dictatorships.

There is also, less creditably, the revival of economic liberalism in social democracy. To be sure, already Bernstein argued for the adoption of the concept of 'individual economic responsibility', even though he admitted the notion came from the 'Manchester School'.[10] And in recent times the most explicit avowal of liberalism and its equation with modern social democracy has been made by the German Social Democratic Party—at one time the citadel of orthodox Marxism. The historic Bad Godesberg Resolution of 1959 is one of the boldest, most impressive 'liberal' party manifestoes ever written. It enunciates as one basic value of socialism the free development of human personality. The struggle, it proclaims, is for the establishment of a society based on human dignity, and it asserts that 'human dignity lies in the claim to individual responsibility'.[11] It considers, further, that free competition and free enterprise are important elements in this new society, and that it is the duty of social democracy to help free enterprise against monopoly, public as well as private. While it recognizes the necessity of some amount of state intervention in today's conditions, its heart clearly lies elsewhere. Its central statement—'Competition as far as it is possible—planning as far as it is necessary'—is as symbolically expressive of the tendency of modern social democracy as some of Marx's or Proudhon's aphorisms were of traditional socialism.

Lastly, we must mention the curious, though perfectly logical, tendency of social democracy to provide an opening for *libertarianism* while showing indifference or even hostility to *egalitarianism*. To repeat: slogans, watch-words should not always be taken at their face value. In their own terms, social democratic leaders (like Hugh Gaitskell, Roy Jenkins and Anthony Crosland in Britain) can be presumed to be genuine in proclaiming 'equality' and 'the classless society' as their aims, though no doubt sometimes 'the amplitude of egalitarian rhetoric' merely serves to mask a retreat even from traditionally held social democratic positions.[12] On analysis, the notion of equality professed by social democrats often turns out to be ambiguous and severely limited. It may refer merely to 'equality of opportunity',[13] or, as in the case of Crosland, to equality which categorically excludes the parity of incomes.[14]

On the other hand, however, many social democrats will boldly press for libertarian reforms. For example, Crosland is most anxious to do away with 'restrictive and puritanical' pressure on the individual, such as the divorce laws, licensing laws, abortion laws, penalties for sexual abnormality and censorship. In the blood of socialists, he asserts, 'there should always run a trace of the anarchist and the libertarian, and not too much of the prig and the prude'.[15] The record, further, of the Wilson administration in Britain in 1964–70 clearly shows this tendency at work. 'Liberal-progressivist' legislation proceeded full scale, while party leaders tended to ignore 'populist' egalitarian demands.[16] The West German Social democrats displayed the same preference in the 1960s. Another telling example here is the record of Swedish social democracy during its long reign. The SAP, as one of its manifestoes declares, has 'invariably' stood up against 'socialization for its own sake', not contemplating total public ownership 'even at a distant date'.[17] At the same time the SAP is most emphatic in denouncing 'conservative moralism' and adopting a 'matter-of-fact conception of man', calling for, amongst other things, the legalization of abortion.[18] In social democratic Sweden, one may remark, there are clear echoes of Fourier not as yet found elsewhere: continuing private ownership with highly advanced welfare provisions and a truly 'libertarian' atmosphere.[19]

Turning now to evaluation, we shall start by making a rather simple-minded but important point: social democracy is certainly not, and does not want to be, Marxism. It is also part of the natural history of Western socialism that it should have gradually divested itself of nearly all traces of Marxism. As Henri de Man said in 1926, vulgar Marxism, i.e. Leninism, was a 'living error'; the 'pure Marxism' of orthodox social democracy was a 'dead truth'.[20] Some parties were never Marxists, others have retained the terminology without the substance.[21] It is then quite obvious that from the Marxist point of view social democracy is not socialism. *If* there is a relentless class-struggle in capitalist society, *if* power must be forcibly wrested from the ruling class, *if* nothing but complete public ownership suffices for the establishment of socialism, *if* the proletariat has the historic destiny to bring about the society of the future, and *if* a dictatorship is necessary in the transitional period, *then* quite clearly social democracy and socialism are poles apart. Marxist commentators have a field-day in denouncing social democrats as 'traitors' to socialism, as petty bourgeois opportunists and lackeys of capitalism: after all, it is undeniable that private ownership has continuously existed in the West; no analysis in terms of a technocratic or managerial revolution can dispute this fact. Also, production here is still undertaken for profit; there is still inequality, 'wage-slavery', and a subordinate working class. The Marxist case, put in these stark theoretical terms, appears very strong indeed.

But social democrats can in turn ask the Marxists themselves: where is Marxism? That is, not Marxism as the abstract analysis of capitalism, but Marxism as a viable practical alternative to social democracy? What, after all, has established Marxism achieved in countries where Marxists are in power? The social democratic position here is in fact rather interesting. While Marxists accuse social democrats of opportunistically seeking accommodation with *existing* capitalism, the latter reverse the same weapon and charge Marxists with actually *establishing* a new kind of 'capitalism' in countries where they succeeded with their revolutions. Already Kautsky denounced early Bolshevik rule in terms which foreshadowed the subsequent social democratic position on this issue. Basing himself on the 'Menshevik' argument that in Russia in 1917 only the remnants of feudalism, but not nascent capitalism, could be overthrown, Kautsky says:

> Today the state bureaucracy and capitalist bureaucracy are consolidated in one body: this is the end result of the great socialist transformation that Bolshevism has accomplished. This signifies the most oppressive of all despotisms in Russia hitherto.[22]

The fact that left-wing critics of the later development of Bolshevism in Russia have had recourse to very similar arguments only adds weight to the social democratic position. The denunciation of established Marxism as 'state capitalism' was later augmented by criticism in terms of managerialism and 'totalitarianism'—corresponding to the new social democratic analysis of Western capitalism. Richard Crossman, for example, has called the Soviet Union 'the most extreme example of managerialism'.[23] And the aforementioned hyper-revisionist Bad Godesberg Resolution minces no words in its condemnation:

> The communists have no right to refer to socialist traditions. In reality they have falsified the content of socialist teaching. Socialists intend to realize freedom and justice, while communists merely utilize social discord with a view to establishing their party's dictatorship.

Apart from appealing to Marxist *fact* with which to refute Marxist *theory*, social democrats can also mount a frontal counter-attack. Why is it obligatory in the first place for socialists to adhere to Marx's teaching? Why does socialism *have* to be Marxism? As we have suggested earlier, at no time has Marxism held a completely dominating position over the whole spectrum of socialism. Today in global terms, of course, Marxism does occupy the centre of the stage. However, it is still far from obvious why it must be accepted to be more relevant to the particular needs of advanced industrial society than social democracy. It is quite clear that the historical pedigree of social democracy and its claim to the name 'socialism' are beyond dispute, hence there is no sense in denying it the 'socialist' label. As the Bad Godesberg Declaration asserts: 'To fight the privileges of the ruling class and to bring about freedom, justice and prosperity for all men— this was and still is the meaning of socialism.' One may legitimately question a number of points in this and similar social democratic assertions, but not the genuine historical links between the social democratic position and old, well-established socialist arguments. Similar sentiments, after all, characterize the writings of Robert Owen, William Thompson, Charles Fourier, the Saint Simonians and Ferdinand Lassalle. In a way perhaps social democracy could be characterized as utopian socialism *minus* utopian expectations: it preaches class co-operation and reconciliation without anticipating the complete disappearance of distinctions, and it preaches ideals like justice, goodwill, brotherliness and compassion without the belief that these could be unreservedly realized. And what is wrong with being 'utopian'? The Marxist claim that utopian socialism represents an 'undeveloped form' of socialism does not today sound entirely convincing. If anything, social democrats can plausibly argue that their espousal of the cause of social justice has had more *actual* working-class support (in advanced societies) than Marxists have had with their doctrine of the class struggle and their endeavours to build up a militant, messianic kind of separate proletarian 'class consciousness'. Concrete examples are furnished by Germany in 1918–23, by Sweden in the inter-war period, and again by West Germany, Britain and Austria in the post-war years.

No doubt, in point of theory social democracy fares badly compared with Marxism. Arguments couched in terms of disembodied 'ideals' do not match up to the comprehensive sweep of the materialist conception of history. Social democratic moralism harks ultimately back to the liberal moral philosophy of Kant (as Bernstein himself declared); Kant, however, had his Hegel. Yet, paradoxical as it may sound, this imperfection gives social democracy a certain kind of appeal. It seems fitted to an imperfect social reality—it is more than an historical accident that the cosiest home of social democracy should have been Great Britain where socialists could always draw on the native tradition of toleration, level-headed empiricism and distrust of abstract theorizing. In Bevan's formulation, the philosophy of social democracy is 'essentially cool in temper'; it succeeds in avoiding absolutes and can thus afford to be 'compassionate and tolerant'. He goes on: 'Consequently it is not able to offer the thrill of the complete abandonment of private judgment, which is the allure of modern Soviet communism and of fascism, its running mate.' [24]

A big question mark must, therefore, accompany all attempts to evaluate social democracy in purely Marxist terms. The least we can do is to endeavour to pass judgment using criteria accepted by social democrats themselves.[25] On this basis our opinion is that social democracy represents a genuine, viable form of socialism, but one which is weak and often prone to degeneration. This weakness, characterizing the moralistic tendency in general, is quite visible in the case of social democracy even in the latter's best form. This best or 'true' form of social democratic majoritarianism can, in the first place, be recognized by the purity of its *aims*. It is true majoritarianism if its concern is really with the establishment of social justice representing the genuine wishes and interests of the underdog, the vast majority of working people. It may give a dull, humdrum, unheroic appearance in many of its day-to-day policies, but then this is the price one pays for the desired goal of general amelioration and the consolidation of gains. In Bevan's fitting words again, social democracy at its best attempts 'to universalize the consumption of the best that society can afford'; cities may not be colourful, but all the children have, or should have, rosy cheeks.[26] Genuine majoritarian policies then must include the vast extension of welfare services and serious efforts to redistribute the wealth of the community by taxation and subsidies, as well as the elevation of public ownership to be the dominant (though not the exclusive) form. It must also include democratization of economic relations by introducing workers' participation in management. All this, of course, needs a comprehensive programme of education, the deliberate inculcation of the (moderate and moralistic!) socialist values of fellowship, cooperation, fairness and fulfilment in creative work.

Secondly, the avowed social democratic *method* of gaining and retaining political power through majoritarianism, by peaceful persuasion, should be given positive appreciation. It represents a clumsy, arduous, roundabout way of proceeding, but one which may often be more successful in the long run. It is interesting to compare and contrast here the stark egalitarian logic of Babouvism (and its derivatives) and the majoritarian logic of social democracy. The former presents the issues in simple terms: existing society oppresses the people; its dominion, however, rests on the passive acquiescence and ignorance of the people themselves; *ergo* society must be overthrown by going against the people's present ideas and desires. For social democracy, on the other hand, justification for action in changing society lies only through successful efforts in persuading the people *now* as to the oppressive nature of the rule under which they have to live. Quite apart from other considerations, social democrats point out that elitist revolutions and governments involve civil war and *continuing* oppression of the people (who will not learn their true interest overnight)—an argument not entirely without the supporting evidence of history. As Durbin warned social democrats, an extremist labour government 'would become a sorry company of deluded Jacobins, fighting a people'.[27]

By the same token, however—such is the nature of the dialectic—it becomes immediately apparent why majoritarianism must represent a weak and limited form of socialism. Through persuasion and popular support you may be able to achieve 'social justice', re-forming the elements of existing capitalist society; but you cannot achieve radical egalitarian changes. As Durbin himself says, a viable programme for the Labour Party is one 'that does not outrage the conservative sections of all classes in this country'.[28] One may quite confidently expect that at one point not only sections, but whole classes, with their entrenched interests and privileges, would be 'outraged' by the promise of radical changes, and would do their utmost to prevent them. Armed intervention and civil war may then easily follow—again, history furnishes examples for this eventuality, too.[29] To deal with this situation, however, one needs a revolutionary egalitarian party, and not a majoritarian social democratic one. Can a social democratic party metamorphose itself into such a body? To this question we shall not venture to give an answer. We may make one comment, however. An egalitarian party needs some measure of support from a non-integrated revolutionary working class. In the West, with its rich texture of social stratification, relative prosperity and cultural homogeneity, this does no longer seem to exist—if the experience of the post-war decades is anything to go by. Advanced industrial society *may* thus have missed the revolutionary bus leading to the egalitarian destination. This is why social democracy seems an eminently fitting form of socialism here. And this is why its appeal has been confined to this society.[30]

Lastly we have also to note the 'impure' shape of social democracy. Just as, in Aristotle, aristocracy can turn into its degenerate form, oligarchy, so social democratic majoritarianism can turn into its degenerate form, which is *electoralism*. This is characterized by the blurring or even losing of long-term socialist objectives, the pragmatic concentration on immediate and unconnected policies, the virtual surrender to underlying status quo forces. It may manifest itself in fetishism of existing social and political institutions, or in a kind of restricted 'rationalism' operating within the capitalist system. No doubt in most instances, as Michael Harrington suggests, the programme 'in which a controlled and managed capitalist growth is seen as a means to socialist ends' 'is a sincere and well-meant illusion'.[31] Sometimes, however, it merely indicates a desire to reach and hold on to political power, the opportunistic substitution of superficial and momentary popularity for the concern for genuine majority needs and interests. To the extent that the pursuit of social justice is prone to fall victim to this kind of degeneration, moralistic socialism stands in constant danger of being engulfed and devoured by the spirit of the age.

7 Rationalism: The European Marxist Establishment

V. I. Lenin succeeded in fusing Marxism with Russian populism, more specifically with the latter's Jacobin variety. In doing this, he inevitably clashed with adherents of orthodox, Western Marxism, both in the Russian social democratic movement and in the Second International. From the strict economic-deterministic viewpoint (into which Western Marxism had developed at the turn of the century), no doubt, Lenin's theories were highly suspect. Disparaging 'objective circumstances' and harshly denouncing the 'worship of spontaneity', Lenin struck an impatient, intolerant, voluntaristic note to which socialism had become unaccustomed. He was not an outstanding philosopher of socialism, but one of the best 'middle-range theorists' the socialist movement has ever produced, as well as, of course, being the victorious founder of the world's first Marxist state. His doctrines and political achievements represent socialism in an overwhelmingly egalitarian style.

Lenin's most striking innovation was in the field of party organization. The concept of the tightly organized 'vanguard' party, the archetype of communist parties the world over, was formulated by him. Two considerations were uppermost in Lenin's mind. Firstly and no doubt correctly, he saw that in a despotic, autocratic country like Tsarist Russia a socialist party could not be organized along open, 'democratic' lines. Secondly, he had doubts about the ability of the working class to raise its revolutionary consciousness within capitalist society. As he puts it in a famous tract:

> The history of all countries shows that the working class, solely by its own forces, is able to work out merely trade-union consciousness, i.e. the conviction of the need for combining in unions, for fighting against the employers, and for trying to prevail upon the government to pass laws necessary for the workers,

etc. The teaching of socialism, however, has grown out of the philosophical, historical and economic theories that were worked out by the educated representatives of the propertied classes— the intelligentsia. The founders of modern scientific socialism, Marx and Engels, themselves belonged by social status to the bourgeois intelligentsia.[1]

However, it is important to note that Lenin's view of the 'intelligentsia' was rather more critical when it came to considering the desirable characteristics of the 'professional revolutionaries' who were to constitute the vanguard party. While intellectuals had been foremost in formulating theories of socialism and teaching the working class, Lenin thought, their 'flabbiness and instability' [2] made them unsuited to work together selflessly, united not by democratic procedures but 'comradely trust', in the service of a common cause. Intellectuals were characterized by 'individualism', bound up with their 'customary mode of life', lacking 'self-training in the spirit of organization and discipline'.[3] On the other hand: 'The proletariat is trained for organization by its whole life, far more radically than many an intellectual prig.' [4] Lenin thus sharply dissociated himself from any openings towards the libertarian tendency, a fact which earned him many critics, but which was largely responsible for the success for his 'Bolshevik' supporters in gaining and retaining power in Russia. As a person, though undoubtedly an 'intellectual' himself, Lenin was also characterized by egalitarian traits: he was devoted, single-minded, modest, with a regular, simple, even ascetic life-style.

His ideal of future society, too, is touchingly, perhaps naïvely, simple, and it is infused by a spirit of classical egalitarianism. Soon after the revolution, Lenin thought, there would be a move 'from formal equality to actual equality', and 'an order under which the functions of control and accounting, becoming more and more simple, will be performed by each in turn, will then become a habit and will finally die out as the *special* functions of a special section of the population.' [5] Like Marx and Engels, he also envisaged the disappearance of the state after the period of the dictatorship of the proletariat, but he indicated that this could come about only if the people had successfully internalized the discipline and solidarity indispensable to freedom in human life. He adhered, that is, to the old Jacobin ideal of the 'one and indivisible republic', putting his faith in the 'voluntary centralism' and 'voluntary fusion of proletarian communes' [6] in the future.

Lenin also advanced a theory of capitalism which became influential, although here he was contributing to an already on-going discussion. Many socialists, including Kautsky, Hilferding, Rosa Luxemburg and the Englishman J. A. Hobson, noted that capitalism was outgrowing the simple 'free-market' model known in the nineteenth century. Lenin, taking his cue from Hobson, asserted that capitalism had reached its highest, 'imperialist' stage, which marked 'the turning-point from the old capitalism to the new, from the domination of capital in general to the domination of finance capital'.[7] Imperialism, Lenin argued, was characterized by the concentration of production, the growth of a financial oligarchy, the appearance of a 'labour aristocracy' in industrialized countries, and the territorial division of the world by the leading capitalist powers. The significance of this view in our perspective is that it shifts the balance of socialist attention away from advanced societies to underdeveloped ones as the most promising *loci* of revolutions. Here another, related, point becomes important. Apart from his unorthodox organizational theories, Lenin also differed from his Menshevik opponents on the role of the peasant masses in Russia. Lenin thought that the peasants could be turned into a decisive revolutionary force with proletarian 'professional' leadership, and that with this united force a deadly blow could be struck against Russia, the 'weakest link' in the world capitalist chain. A victorious socialist (and not merely bourgeois) revolution in an underdeveloped country, that is, would be the detonator of world-wide revolution. The vistas this view opened up for socialism were tremendous, and the subsequent concentration of revolutionary egalitarian tendencies in poor and ex-colonial countries is just as much of an historical illustration of Lenin's foresight as is the diminution of socialism in the Western world.

To use a hackneyed phrase then, Lenin appears as a transitional figure, in two important senses. Here, of course, 'transitional' signifies the very opposite of understating his role. On the one hand, his emphasis on the revolutionary potentials of underdevelopment and his global view of capitalism mark the transition from European socialism to socialism in Asia, Africa and Latin America—in the next chapter we shall have more to say on this. On the other hand, more relevantly here, Lenin is also the transition from the early egalitarian momentum of Russian Marxism to its subsequent rationalist development. Lenin and the Bolshevik leadership, after their successful *coup* in October 1917, were for some years anticipating an early spread of the revolution

Socialism

to West European states. This expectation, just as the social democrats' belief in socialist parliamentary majorities, was unfulfilled. The
Bolsheviks thus were forced to concentrate on *Realpolitik*: having
successfully destroyed counter-revolutionary forces (as well as Leftist
opposition), they had to set about organizing the government of Russia.
Lenin's famous quip about communism being the combination of
'soviets' and 'electrification' symbolized the precarious unity of egalitarianism and rationalism, and his 'New Economic Policy' of compromise with private enterprise signalled the first step towards modi-
fication of the egalitarian goal. Lenin also, at the Seventh Congress
of the Communist Party (1918), set up the Politburo and the Secre-
tariat, thus, at least in principle, opening the way to bureaucratization.
His untimely death in 1924 and his personal dislike of Stalin may lead
one to ask if under him Russia would not have developed differently;
however, this is not a question which we could profitably explore
here.

The consolidation of Bolshevik rule in Russia, which in political
terms meant Stalin's ascendancy and his speedy elimination of all
leadership rivals, had many illustrious victims from among the old
revolutionary guard, and none more colourful than the irrepressible
Lev Davidovich (Leon) Trotsky. At first a Menshevik, Trotsky became
Lenin's second in command in 1917, and his role in the *coup* as well as
in the ensuing protracted civil war was outstanding. Yet his eclipse
later is not entirely incomprehensible. Trotsky was not at home in the
arena of practical cloak-and-dagger politics, and he was no match for
Stalin. Besides, he was too much of an uncompromising, somewhat
even dogmatic, Leftist, who was unhappy with the chameleon changes
and turns of Bolshevik policy. Steadfast in his belief in a European
revolution and the 'crisis' of international capitalism, Trotsky vehemently opposed Stalin's notion of 'socialism in one country', believing
this to be a 'reactionary utopia'.[8] To this idea he opposed his famous
theory of 'permanent revolution', the view that in underdeveloped
countries (like Russia) the proletariat was the only class capable of
assuming the leadership in the fight for the socialist revolution. In his
own words:

> With regard to countries with a belated bourgeois development,
> especially the colonial and semi-colonial countries, the theory of
> the permanent revolution signifies that the complete and genuine
> solution of their tasks of achieving *democracy and national*

emancipation is conceivable only through the dictatorship of the proletariat as the leader of the subjugated nation, above all its peasant masses.[9]

While this conception certainly appears to have an orthodox Marxist pedigree, and is in line with Lenin's policies in 1917, it is not entirely in accord with all that Lenin wrote (as Stalin's ideologues and independent scholars had no difficulty in pointing out).[10] It is worth noting here that Trotsky in the 1920s fully accepted Lenin's view of the vanguard party, which, of course, *was* for all intents and purposes the 'proletariat'.[11] And as an historian has said, 'Trotsky during the critical period of the struggle always attacked Stalin for pursuing wrong policies, never for applying wrong principles of party discipline to enforce them.'[12]

It was after he fell from power, and subsequent to his expulsion from Russia in 1929, that Trotsky developed his critique of Stalinist Bolshevism as leading to the bureaucratic 'degeneration of the workers' state'. Accusing Stalin of having 'betrayed the revolution', Trotsky asserted: 'Stalinism re-established the most offensive forms of privileges, imbued inequality with a provocative character, strangled mass self-activity under police absolutism, transformed administration into a monopoly of the Kremlin oligarchy and regenerated the fetishism of power . . .'[13] Trotsky's followers in Russia, as Trotsky claimed, 'were fighting for the interests of the international revolution and thus setting ourselves against the conservatism of the bureaucracy and its longing for tranquillity, prosperity, and comfort.'[14] Significantly, however, Trotsky continued to look upon Russia as a genuine 'workers' state', enslaved only by the workers' own bureaucracy, but not by a new 'class'. (Admitting the existence of a new exploitative 'class', of course, creates considerable theoretical problems for Marxism, as witness the subsequent scholastic debates among later critics of Stalinism, many of them claiming to be Trotsky's disciples.)

Trotsky's was a tragic fate, and by no means merely on account of his being murdered by an assassin. He was one of the most brilliant, sophisticated Marxist thinkers, and his unflagging revolutionary zeal was matched by his extremely acute and manysided theoretical refinements of Marxism. Yet all the time he was moving within a well-nigh unbreakable glasshouse of fanaticism, and events left him behind. His figure and doctrines, of course, still inspire a relatively small but dedicated group of Marxists whose relentless denunciation of 'official' communism and whose grassroots revolutionary activism in advanced capitalist countries have at times been influential. Trotskism is among the most important indigenous forms of egalitarian socialism still extant in the West today. However, the Trotskists' fetishism of the 'working class' and their never-ending internecine quarrels often make them impotent and even antiquated in a Western context. Their influence in the underdeveloped world has not proved very fertile so far.

I. V. Stalin, on the other hand, was not left behind by events: he made them happen. He is one of the key figures of twentieth-century socialism, and the controversy surrounding his name should not deter us from attempting to see him in perspective. After his near-beatification in his life-time, Stalin became the devil incarnate in the eyes of critics and many advocates of socialism alike, the convenient bogey figure whom everyone can attack easily, without compunction. ('Stalinism' in this respect is somewhat akin to South African 'apartheid' which liberals, social democrats, Christians, conservatives can denounce without any embarrassment.) Now it is not our purpose to 'whitewash' or exonerate Stalin in any important moral sense. But in order to facilitate better understanding, we shall draw a distinction between two layers of Stalinism; these we might call respectively 'overt' or 'methodological' and 'covert' or 'substantive' Stalinism.

Most critics when they denounce Stalin—not excluding his actual heirs in Russia—concentrate only on 'overt' Stalinism. No one can blame them, since the list of Stalin's 'crimes' is notoriously long and spine-chilling. Just to mention a few of the most well-known events and policies attaching to Stalin's name: the forced collectivization of agriculture in Russia (which had, however, been Trotsky's policy before Stalin himself turned 'Left'); his cunning and murderous elimination of his rivals from the Bolshevik leadership; his treatment of anarchists and Trotskists in the Spanish Civil War; his show trials and bloody purges; his labour-camps, the now proverbial 'Gulag Archipelago'; his maintaining a reign of universal terror, suspicion, stagnation, after the Second World War extended to East European countries; his anti-Semitism; his cruelty in private life; etc., etc. And quite apart from his 'crimes', Stalin seems also to have made some major political 'mistakes'; here one could mention his China policy, his unpreparedness at the time of the Nazi attack on Russia in 1941, his Yugoslavia policy, and his isolationism and neglect of the Third World in the Cold War period. Add to all this the repellent and nauseating 'cult' which grew up around his person, his self-elevation to be the absolute God-the-father of world socialism (backed, unlike the Pope, by real battalions), and the widespread revulsion (or at least acute unease) which his name evokes almost everywhere will be readily comprehensible.

Yet this is not the end of the story. It is remarkable that it took Stalin's followers (by which one does not mean political leaders in Russia only, but Marxist 'intellectuals' elsewhere as well) some *years* after Stalin's death in 1953 to free themselves from the dead dictator's shadow. This suggests that the shadow could not have been cast by an unsubstantial body. No naked force and no sheer wickedness can keep a movement enthralled for over twenty years; no nonentity and no cynical career politician could ever build up a faintly comparable 'personality cult'. In truth, Stalin was a world-historical individual whose achievements, for better or worse, proved lasting. It is a small but not entirely insignificant point, though often overlooked today, that in his life Stalin had real popularity with the masses in Russia, especially during the 'Great Patriotic War': for many ordinary people 'Comrade Stalin' represented the living unity of the Tsar's fatherly care of his people and the revolutionary leader's more rational and palpable appeal.[15] People have, of course, often been deceived by leaders; in this case, however, deception and terror cannot furnish a complete explanation.

This leads us to what has been termed 'covert' or 'substantive' Stalinism. The core of Stalin's achievement is the construction of the *rationalist state*. His methods no doubt raise very important moral questions. But the overall strategic aims for which these methods were employed should not on this account be left to oblivion. In our perspective, at any rate, these substantive aims are more relevant, for the following all-important reason: in this sense of 'Stalinism' the subsequent period, far from succeeding in 'destalinization', has only built further on foundations which Stalin laid down. The concrete facts of Stalin's economic reconstruction and development of Russia are well known, and we need make only brief references to them. Besides the collectivization of agriculture (which proved to be a mixed blessing), Stalin brought about the industrialization of Russia, achieving an annual growth rate which was unprecedented in modern times. Whether or not this could have been accomplished using milder political methods is ultimately an unanswerable question. The result was, at any rate, that Russia became one of the leading industrial countries of the world. Of even greater importance here, however, is the overall economic *pattern* which developed as a result of Stalin's policies. For the first time in history, a large and potentially rich state introduced a well-nigh completely centralized system of economic planning for the running of its industries. Stalin's five-year-plans, while causing a great deal of suffering and running into difficulties with the passing of time, led nevertheless out of the chaos and poverty of the post-revolutionary era: they were, not unjustly, objects of admiration by socialists everywhere.[16] A vast and intricate hierarchical system of economic decision-making developed correspondingly to central planning; while the overall political control remained in the hands of the communist party apparatus—Stalin's own creation—increasingly more importance became attached to technical expertise and organizational ability: Stalin's system needed, and duly generated, an influential group of industrial managers, engineers, scientists, economic experts of all kinds.

The socialist ideology which Stalin put forward is explicable in the light of his system's basic orientation towards the increase of production and the modernization of Russia's economy. Stalin introduced a system of high income differentials and encouraged material incentives. He contemptuously dismissed egalitarianism: '. . . every Leninist knows, if he is a real Leninist, that equalization in the sphere of requirements and personal, everyday life is a reactionary petty-bourgeois absurdity worthy of some primitive sect of ascetics, but not of a socialist society . . .'[17] He wanted to build socialism not on 'the basis of poverty and privation', but 'on the basis of a vigorous growth of the productive forces of society', leading to 'the full and all-round satisfaction of all the requirements of culturally developed working people'.[18] These statements were made in 1934, at the very beginning of the Stalin era. After the War, it seems, Stalin's inegalitarian convictions became even stronger. It was he who, shortly before his death, began to emphasize the fact that the Soviet socialist economy was still subject to the 'law of value'—in itself not a shattering revelation, but significant in the light of Stalin's economic policies. These were already quite visibly leading to subsequent changes which posterity has too often been ready to attribute to 'destalinization'. It was Stalin himself who declared that in the production of consumer goods 'such things as cost accounting and profitableness, production costs, prices, etc. are of actual importance in our enterprises'.[19] In 1952 he claimed the 'basic economic law of socialism' to be:

. . . the securing of the maximum satisfaction of the constantly rising material and cultural requirements of the whole of society through the continuous expansion and perfection of socialist production on the basis of higher techniques.[20]

This is a clear and unambiguous statement of rationalism—it could directly have come out of Saint-Simon. Except that—and this is what confuses the observer—Stalin's role did remain fundamentally ambiguous: there is an unmistakable contradiction between 'overt' and 'covert' Stalinism. Stalin's methods may just possibly and in part have been excusable if they had served genuinely *egalitarian* ends; at any rate, they would have had then a more coherent logical pattern. Or, as a rationalist, Stalin may just conceivably have had recourse later to other policies, more in line with rationalist development, the course which in fact his followers have opted for. Stalin was, then, Robespierre and the Directorate rolled into one—dubious, but still a distinction. In the words of a recent commentator: 'Although the Soviet communist movement undoubtedly underwent very considerable deradicalization during the Stalin era, Stalin himself, a man of the original revolutionary generation, represented in his peculiar way a link with the radical Leninist past and a bar to *full-scale* development of the deradicalizing tendencies that had become strong in Soviet communism.' [21]

Changes and dislocations followed Stalin's demise. The long-term development towards a fuller form of rationalism was often derailed and held up. Discontent with overt Stalinism was too strong, the forces of modernization often too impatient, the old-style Stalinists too afraid to lose their power and accept responsibility for their misdeeds. The Soviet leaders took some positive steps in order to end their global isolation. Yugoslavia, where Tito's communists had enjoyed popular support and which had embarked on a rationalist course long before the rest of Eastern Europe, had been ostracized by Stalin: now there was a promise of reconciliation. Many of Stalin's old associates in Russia were eliminated from power. The new leader, Nikita Khrushchev, had been Stalin's chief party secretary in the Ukraine; now, however, he became the pioneer of destalinization, and it was his secret speech to the historic Twentieth Congress of the Soviet party which set the tone for subsequent changes and rationalizations of Soviet policy. Under Khrushchev the Soviet Union began to tackle more seriously the two outstanding economic problems bequeathed by the Stalin era: agriculture and consumer goods. Investment in heavy industry was slowed down and steps were taken to raise living standards—policies which Stalin himself might well have inaugurated. There was, however, also a growth in 'socialist legality' and curbing of the powers of the security organs; the old atmosphere of siege, mobilization and terror was slowly lifting; there were cautious attempts to ungag literature and the arts.

In the mid-fifties, however, a serious jolt in Eastern Europe all but halted the process, or so it was thought at the time. Russia's dependencies had had, in some ways, a harder time under Stalin than the Soviet Union itself: here (except in Yugoslavia and Albania) there had been no indigenous egalitarian revolutions, but Stalin's ironclad rationalism had been imposed by the Soviet army and maintained by local potentates who had little popular support. Thus destalinization was a more traumatic experience and it brought forth movements which seriously jeopardized the regional Soviet system. Riots and a change of government and communist party leadership in Poland were followed, in October 1956, by a large-scale uprising in Hungary the defeat of which necessitated the involvement of Soviet tanks and troops. The Hungarian rising, provoked by a particularly shortsighted Stalinist leadership, was led by national-minded socialist forces whose aim was the establishment of a wider-based, decentralized, indeed a more 'rationalist' socialist system, with a prominent role allotted to workers' councils. As the rising gathered momentum, however, these forces were joined by other elements, leading to the proclamation of policies (e.g. withdrawal from the Warsaw Pact) which made it easier for an at first hesitant Soviet leadership to intervene. The Western powers' imperialistic Suez adventure was also an operative factor. Thus by the late fifties it seemed that there might be a return to overt Stalinism.

But in fact the rationalizing process was going on, and in retrospect it might be said that the aforementioned temporary setbacks only strengthened the underlying long-term tendencies. The Khrushchev era saw the Soviet Union become richer, more powerful, and more respected the world over: technological advance, symbolized by Sputnik and Gagarin's space-flight, was coupled with seeking genuine rapprochement with the West and a more positive attitude taken towards rising nationalist forces in the Third World. The Soviet Union itself was now beginning to experiment with partial economic decentralization: Liberman's economic theories were gaining respectability and some measure of official approval. More ominously, and to some extent as a direct result of these changes themselves, Russia and China began to draw apart. Khrushchev's decision to withdraw Soviet technicians added to the Chinese displeasure felt over Russian destalinization and her growing moderation in the international field. The Sino-Soviet conflict, of course, cannot be explained in ideological terms alone: the national interest of the two great powers has also played an important role.

The Soviet communist party programme, which was accepted by the Twenty-second Congress in 1962 (the high-tide of destalinization), spelt out the changes in Russian thinking clearly, giving formal expression to Khrushchev's policies. Thus it declares that in the present era the achievement of international socialism is no longer necessarily connected with war, and that it is the objective of Marxism-Leninism to work for this goal by peaceful means. The document also acknowledges the existence of 'national democracy' in developing countries, that is, an alliance of 'progressive' forces, including but not led by the communists, fighting against imperialism and neo-colonialism. Significantly, while the programme still uses the revolutionary Marxist term, the 'dictatorship of the proletariat', in connection with newly established socialist systems, in respect of the Soviet Union itself it claims that the state organization has reached a higher level. 'The state which arose as a state of the dictatorship of the proletariat, has in the new, contemporary stage, become a state of the entire people, an organ expressing the interests and will of the people as a whole.'[22] Now while this definition may be indicative of mellower, more peaceful relations of government within the Soviet Union (replacing Stalin's state of permanent vigilance and emergency), one must note at the same time its revisionist character from the orthodox Marxist point of view. As Isaac Deutscher has pointed out, this definition of the state closely resembles the Lassallean conception of the socialist 'people's state'.[23]

The document confidently awaits the arrival of full 'communism' in the foreseeable future. It is, however, of paramount importance to note that the definition of communism here has a markedly rationalist flavour. The programme emphasizes that in communism 'the all-round development of people will be accompanied by the growth of productive forces through continuous progress in science and technology'.[24] Further, it expects people to have 'a high degree of communist consciousness, industry, discipline and devotion to the public interest'.[22] Communism 'alters the character of work, but it does not release the members of society from work. It will by no means be a society of anarchy, idleness and inactivity.' 'Communism represents the highest form of organization of public life.'[26] There is overwhelming emphasis on technical progress and prosperity; it is pointed out that in the future Soviet people will be more prosperous than those living in capitalist countries, although their individual income will be more equal on average. There will be no parasitical classes as there are in capitalism. Finally the programme reaffirms what it calls 'Lenin's thesis' and what is the clearest indication of rationalism as the leading principle of Soviet communism:

> The Party acts upon Lenin's thesis that communist construction must be based upon the principle of material incentive. In the coming twenty years payment according to one's work will remain the principal source for satisfying the material and cultural needs of the working people.[27]

Khrushchev's fall from power in 1964 did not, although again there were uncertainties, lead to any significant changes in the general direction of Soviet and East European development. The Brezhnyev-Kosygin leadership, though harder on the intellectuals, continued the slow process of economic reorganization. Lately there has been an attempt further to increase the efficiency and economic viability of state enterprises by the creation of large 'production associations'— the equivalent (almost) of the giant Western capitalist 'corporations'.[28] In East European countries the rationalizing process has been taken even further. In Hungary, the 'new economic mechanism' has led to an upsurge of production and trade (with COMECON as well as Western countries), but also, not entirely unexpectedly, to a rise in the cost of living. As usual, Yugoslavia has again blazed the rationalist trail and experienced the consequences in the acutest form: here economic reforms, devaluation, deflation and unemployment have had in the mid-sixties, according to an observer, 'savagely paleo-capitalist effects'.[29] On the political front, the Sino-Soviet conflict went from bad to worse, at one time even involving armed border clashes between the two countries. Roumania, a faithful ally of the Soviet Union for a long time, now struck out on a bold course of independent foreign policy, 'mediating' between Russia and China, and achieving a rapprochement with the Western powers. She has not, however, experimented with radical economic and political changes, internally retaining more than others the inherited centralistic pattern (even becoming more centralistic and nationalistic with regard to minorities).

Fresh disturbances, however, occurred in three other countries in the late sixties. In Czechoslovakia the new party leadership under Dubcek embarked on a course of 'liberalization', renouncing the party's hegemony of power and encouraging pluralism in the media; [30] added impetus was given to further economic changes through official sponsorship of Ota Sik's unorthodox doctrines. This departure, as is well known, was foiled by the Warsaw Pact countries' armed intervention in August 1968. In Yugoslavia, students led public demonstrations against growing inequality and privileges, denouncing the 'red bourgeoisie' and forcing Tito into accepting reforms. In Poland, the combined effect of student disturbances and workers' active protests against a steeply rising cost of living resulted in the replacement of Gomulka (in the fifties the symbol of destalinization and 'national communism') by Gierek and a new rationalistic, 'technocratic' administration. Apart, however, from these and similar, though smaller, dislocations, the underlying trend towards gradual rationalist reorganization and general prosperity has continued. In a global context, the Soviet Union and the European Marxist establishment as a whole unquestionably represent forces of stability today, pulling in their wake West European Communist parties whose political profile now in Western countries increasingly brings them nearer to the social democratic left. New eruptions, of course, might always occur—upheavals and leadership changes in the past could not have been predicted either. But the odds are that the pattern of past decades will be repeated: bold attempts at innovation leading to repression in the short run, but not making any appreciable difference to the long-term process.

We may now venture to make some remarks, reducing of necessity an extremely complex situation surrounded by political and academic controversy to something like a comprehensible general picture. Needless to say, just as in the case of social democracy, here too individual national differences between countries in the region render all attempts at generalization rather problematic. Bearing this in mind, however, we may plausibly characterize the socialism of the European Marxist establishment as being predominantly rationalistic, in the sense of affording highest priority to the goals of material prosperity, economic efficiency and individual satisfaction, hence encouraging societal development in an expert-oriented, meritocratic direction.[31]

In this perspective, we have suggested, the differences between centralism and bureaucratic control in the Stalin era and the partial decentralization *cum* vestigial militancy prevalent today are not as important
as their underlying similarities: both can be seen as succeeding stages
of the same process. There is, of course, no historical necessity involved
in all this: the metamorphosis of militant egalitarianism into staid
rationalism over the years was not foreordained, and we would not be
entitled to infer that this pattern would have to be reproduced elsewhere. Nonetheless, as regards Russia and Eastern Europe, one can
pinpoint certain factors which in retrospect make this particular kind
of development comprehensible.

In brief it seems that rationalism in this region has been the outcome
of the historical conjuncture of a certain stage of economic development and given traditional patterns of social and political relationships
and attitudes. The stage of economic development reached is one
beyond primary accumulation and the establishment of basic mechan-
ized industries. Of traditional thought and behaviour patterns one
should make special mention of the deep-lying conservatism of the
peoples living in this region. Multi-level modernization has not gone
much beyond the surface. There is still great respect for authority as
such, and people habitually look to the state, to the highest organ of the
community, for justice and the melioration of their life-conditions. Not
so long ago, we may recall, this region was ruled over by autocratic
empires: Ottoman, Romanov, Habsburg, Hohenzollern (the German
Democratic Republic comprises a large part of Prussia). There never
was here a bourgeois or liberal revolution: reforms as well as revolutions were handed down from above. Rationalist socialism, therefore,
could fit in smoothly with the inherited authoritarian background,
becoming more illiberal than it need have been. Nationalism, too, has
here often tended to reinforce conservative attitudes. Further, there
seems to be a strong grain of individualist materialism, influencing
economic (and by implication political) behaviour. It has, of course, a
rationale: the long-standing poverty of the people in the region has
been greatly aggravated by their having been exposed to the intellectual products of Western bourgeois culture, thus turning them into the
envious poor relations of their wealthier Western neighbours. The
individualism which grew up here thus became more impatient, more
thrusting, much less tolerant or self-limiting. In the region as a whole
there has developed something like a spirit of capitalism without the
protestant ethic. And as Henri de Man has astutely observed, 'the

rule of capitalism means something very different from the rule of the capitalist class; it depends upon the fact that every one would like to be a capitalist, that every one feels and thinks as a capitalist.'[32]

At first glance, therefore, one might be tempted to say that a possible 'restoration of capitalism' or 'creeping capitalism' presents here a real danger. Inherited possessiveness and thwarted acquisitiveness may well be reinforced and given free rein by the institutional developments we have mentioned. Inequality and relatively high income and status differentials do now exist in all countries in the area; there is also decentralization and growing emphasis on direct material incentives; ownership of personal effects (including houses and motor cars) is encouraged and private enterprise in certain small-scale industries is actively tolerated; moreover, there has been an influx of Western capital.[33] It may be misleading or premature to talk in terms of an emerging 'new class' of bureaucrats or industrial managers, either collectively or individually 'owning' the means of production: what is more interesting to observe is the close similarity of ideological arguments justifying this process to views formulated in the West at the dawn of the capitalist era. There was, for example, a clear echo of Adam Smith's 'invisible hand' in Liberman's justification of autonomy for state enterprises:

> , . . . the proposed system proceeds from the principle: what is profitable for society must be profitable for each enterprise. And conversely, what is unprofitable for society must be extremely unprofitable for the collective of any enterprise.[34]

Even if capitalism is not restored in the narrow institutional sense, one might argue, it can still be smuggled in under a different guise and parading a seemingly novel institutional structure. What does appear certain is that the earlier egalitarian momentum of socialist movements has not been able to achieve a decisive breakthrough: the spirit of the age has again proved stronger than expected.

The numerous attempts at 'liberalization' could perhaps be understood in this light. These attempts have followed from underlying economic transformation, and their aim has been to achieve greater ideological coherence in the political life of these countries. It would appear so from a rather diluted Marxist point of view, too: if the economic base takes up a more pluralistic (i.e. decentralized) shape, one can expect the political, etc. superstructure to follow suit. Thus demands for greater political diversity, free and public criticism, a spirit of general toleration, are effects thrown up by the *natural* evolution of these systems themselves: they are not, or at least not directly, ideological imports of Western liberalism or manifestations of an eternal 'human nature'. It might be thought that the most desirable way of future development lies through the checking of tendencies leading towards capitalist restoration, while simultaneously accelerating political liberalization. Many people, including the Yugoslav students whose demands in 1968 reflected a combination of Maoist and 'Djilasist' (liberal-social democratic) ideas,[35] have hitched their hopes on to an evolution of this kind. But this seems to be little more than wishful thinking: the inherent conflict between egalitarianism and community on the one hand, and individualism and diversity on the other,[36] is not much nearer to resolution and synthesis today in Eastern Europe than it has been at any other time.

However, we must also bear in mind that the so-called 'danger of capitalist restoration' might just be due to one's misunderstanding the nature of *socialism*. We have, of course, argued all along that socialism ought not to be sharply distinguished from capitalism or liberalism, but that we should recognize soft or moderate tendencies in socialism which differ from certain features of modern capitalist society only in degree. Rationalism is such a moderate tendency. One thing we could say about it here, on the basis of East European experience, is that it is a vigorous, self-sufficient tendency, more so than moralism which prevails in Western social democracy. Rationalism, it seems, can stand on its own feet. After all, the rationalist development of socialism merely represents what liberal capitalism itself has always wanted to be, namely a society geared to the most efficient production of material goods with the objective of the maximization of human happiness. So it might not be altogether absurd to suggest that in the long run the attraction of rationalist socialism can be stronger than the corresponding pull of capitalism. Whether today's Soviet and East European leaders are seen as a new 'class' or just a 'stratum', they do appear to have sufficient vigour, resilience, single-mindedness and clarity of purpose to carry through their designs to the full. Besides, one must not overlook the fact that, discrepancies and blemishes notwithstanding, rationalism here has built on egalitarian and moralistic advances in such fields as welfare, education and the fostering of community feeling. Even if there is a new stratification under way, the shake-up of the traditional class structures has resulted in a fermentation which is likely, in the long run, to lead to developments at least intellectually more exciting than are present prospects in the West. Rationalist socialism is brash, harsh, intolerant, illiberal, but it has every chance of maturing and thereby humanizing itself; recent advances in learning and in the arts as well as growing prosperity are at least signs pointing that way.

Obviously, tremendous importance attaches here to manifestations of the *moralist* tendency of socialism which in this context has the task of making the rationalist establishment mellower, more humane. It may not turn out to be more of an impracticable undertaking than the task facing moralism in the West. The ever more courageous stand taken by leading intellectuals in recent years over such questions as 'human rights', 'legality', 'justice' and 'decency' is proving a fertile influence. It is now supported by wider sections of society than before. Thus although, as we have suggested, it would be wrong to expect perfection (in the sense of the synthesis of various tendencies), the future coexistence of rationalism and moralism is not entirely beyond the bounds of possibility.

8 Egalitarianism: The Lean and Hungry Socialists

There must be some audacity involved in any attempt to discuss social-ism in the Third World in general terms. The difficulties which we have encountered in connection with social democracy and European Marxism apply here in an augmented sense: there is not one socialism in the Third World but several, and variation among countries is much more prominent than in the 'First' and 'Second' Worlds. Com-pared to the vast continents of the Third World, its hundreds of millions of inhabitants belonging to the widest variety of cultures and stages of economic development, the problems of social democracy appear parochial, those of European Marxism somewhat claustrophobic. At the same time, however, the problems of the Third World con-verge on fundamental issues whose urgency and importance easily surpass problems encountered elsewhere: here socialism is directly, immediately relevant to all basic human concerns. In this chapter we shall briefly state what appear to be among the most prominent com-mon features of socialism in the Third World; then we shall discuss the experience of China and Cuba at somewhat greater length, since these two countries offer the best examples for the underlying tendency which seems to characterize what is most interesting and most dis-tinctive about Third World socialism as a whole.

The first and simplest thing to note is that socialism in the Third World is represented by, and advanced on behalf of, people who are 'hungry' and 'lean'. They are hungry, poverty-stricken, miserable, standing in many cases on the brink of starvation. The wealth and comfort concentrated in Europe and North America have strange echoes here among the millions of underfed, emaciated Asians, Africans, Latin Americans. They are also 'lean' in the sense of being relatively unburdened by the quantity of intellectual fat accompanying the prosperity of Western nations, affecting also Western socialism. It more or less follows that the predominant tendency of socialism here should be *egalitarian,* with all the drive and dynamism as well as the less palatable features of this tendency. The two main character-istics of egalitarianism, as we defined it in Chapter Two, are present: a strong feeling of community coupled with a rejection of Western individualism, and a clear conception of conflict between sharply defined antagonists, the native populations of the Third World on one side, the Western ex-colonial powers and their representatives on the other. The cultural, national, linguistic and sometimes racial distinc-tions between the 'white' West and North and the 'coloured' East and South, only accentuate a conflict which has had its origins in uneven economic development and resultant exploitation.

For the same reason socialist thought here is on the whole simple, hard-hitting, straightforward, emotional, often hardly more than a string of slogans, denunciations, imperatives—with a few notable exceptions, of course. But generally it would be fair to say that in the Third World one witnesses a process of *desophistication* of socialism. The point to make about this process is that it is by no means a wholly undesirable kind of development, as far as socialism is concerned, con-trary to what many Western observers, over-intellectualized and imbued with the importance of theory, seem to feel.[1] What desophisti-cation signifies is the fact that in the Third World socialism is con-cerned with simple, everyday issues, with tasks that are both vital and immediate, having unquestionable priority as well as being within the grasp of impoverished, uneducated masses—such as the tasks of food-production and distribution, the creation of industry, the formation of political consciousness, the achievement and preservation of inde-pendence. There is in the Third World, one might suggest, a much more convincing 'unity of theory and practice' in socialism than there ever was in Europe, except perhaps at the height of revolutions. It is, further, only to be expected that such a convergence has to be pur-chased at the price of intellectual descent: the urgency and immediacy of practice must be matched by the simplicity and blunt conciseness of theory.

Secondly, as has been noted by practically all students of Third World politics, socialism here is closely linked to *nationalism.* Now we have already made the suggestion earlier in this book that national-ism in theoretical terms could well be regarded as an arrested form of socialism, and that in practice it could be either an ally or an enemy to socialism. In the Third World it is pre-eminently an ally, for reasons which we can briefly indicate. Firstly, it is to be remembered that the

Third World is a 'world' only in the passive sense, having been created by Western colonialism and imperialism. Its peoples, therefore, in order to become active participants in a really *new* world, have as their principal task the reassertion or rediscovery of a group-identity which had been completely lost or suffered humiliation during the era of colonial dependency. Western radicals and socialists can afford to be fully 'international' in outlook, since in their case national identity—in the sense of being partakers of mature, emancipated cultures—is no longer a problem, and it certainly appears unconnected with the task of social and economic emancipation. But in the Third World the achievement of a lesser group-consciousness is and must be the expression also of socialist aspirations.[2] Even accepting, secondly, the Marxist definition of nationalism as bourgeois or petty bourgeois ideology, one can argue that in a Third World context this makes different sense: here classes themselves, having been created in the anti-colonialist struggle, find new historical roles waiting for them. The telescoping of progress in time means also its contraction in terms of social space. But more of this later. For now let us just add the remark that the (to a large extent justifiable) revulsion felt by many Western socialists towards 'nationalism' is also due to a rigid, reductionist understanding of this concept. In truth nationalism is no less of an 'open texture' than socialism: there is no sharp dividing line between 'group-identity' or 'patriotism' on the one hand, and 'nationalism' or 'chauvinsim' on the other. One must condemn excesses and malformations (e.g. an opening towards racialism which is hardly an insuperable problem in Third World socialism), but one must not be oblivious to the ground-level connections which exist between group-consciousness and the egalitarian tendency in socialism.

One more general point needs to be made. The Third World is culturally most complex and heterogeneous. Its peoples have their own traditions, often very different from those associated with Western civilization. It is quite obvious hence that socialism here will feed also on cultural roots different from the ones included in our overall framework. Indeed, Third World socialist leaders have often claimed the special significance for socialism of their own non-European cultural traditions; and moreover it is undeniable that in some cases, notably Gandhian pacifist socialism, these non-European roots have had considerable trans-cultural influence. In general, however, it would be safe to assert that Third World socialist ideologies with indigenous roots fall into the anti-liberal category, that is, they tend to be moralistic or egalitarian.

They are almost unanimous in rejecting Western-type individualism. With 'Arab socialism', for example, the Islamic religious tradition of social cohesion and the effacement of the individual is often stressed. With 'African socialism' the emphasis is usually laid on traditional tribal consciousness and social conventions, with particular reference to the intimate relationship the African had with his fellows and inanimate nature before the onset of European colonization. As the eminent statesman and philosopher, Leopold Senghor, has expressed it, 'in contrast to the classic European, the Negro-African does not draw a line between himself and the object'. And in the words of Julius Nyerere: 'We, in Africa, have no more need of being "converted" to socialism than we have of being "taught" democracy. Both are rooted in our own past—in the traditional society which produced us. Modern African socialism can draw from its traditional heritage the recognition of "society" as an extension of the basic family unit.' In the words of Tom Mboya, African socialism refers to 'those proved codes of conduct in African societies which have, over the ages, conferred dignity on our people and afforded them security regardless of their station in life'. He also lays special emphasis on the 'universal charity' which characterized traditional African society, and on the African's 'thought processes and cosmological ideas which regard man not as a social means, but as an end and entity in the society'.[3]

We may then, it seems, venture the suggestion that although non-European traditions *are* often important, they are not (in our perspective) entirely indispensable as a part of explanation: what is most striking and most dynamic in the socialism of the Third World is amenable to a characterization in terms of the egalitarian tendency of socialism, the tendency which grows out of *classical*, pre-Christian and pre-individualist, Western roots. The dynamic traits of Third World socialism indicate not so much the presence of non-European roots, but the revival of the original impetus behind egalitarian socialism in the aftermath of the great French Revolution: today's situation is the global replica of the erstwhile crystal-clear confrontation between the rich and poor, the privileged and the exploited. It is not too far-fetched to argue even that Third World socialism actually enhances its impact, and its militant egalitarianism, precisely to the extent that it assumes the classical mantle and assigns other traditions a more subordinate role.

A telling example here is Frantz Fanon, the Negro thinker whose revolutionary ideas were forged mainly in the crucible of the Algerian people's fight for independence. Fanon is the most extreme, uncompromising enemy of Western colonialism, yet he is also the thinker whose doctrines bear most visibly the European imprint. His intellectual origins are in Rousseau, Marx, Sorel, Freud and Sartre. What is most widely known about Fanon's views by the general public, however, might not be the most significant. It is his harsh views on the white European settler and his belief in the 'cleansing force' of violence which tend to hit the academic headlines. But in Fanon these are based on a rounded philosophy of the effects of colonization. This he saw as a process leading to the destruction of the very humanity of colonial peoples, giving rise to a system incomparably harsher than capitalism. In the former, the non-European native is oppressed by sheer force; there are no mediating moral and ideological relations as there are in capitalism within the same culture. Thus here more is involved in the struggle than the conventional goals of socialism. As Fanon wrote, here 'the fight for national dignity gives its true meaning to the struggle for bread and social dignity'. And: 'The colonized have this in common, that their right to constitute a people is challenged.' [4] And so 'for the native, life can only spring up again out of the rotting corpse of the settler'; [5] independence as a gift of the colonial power is valueless; the native's inferiority complex can only be obliterated through violent resistance and struggle.

Fanon argues that the system replacing colonial dependence would have to be socialist. His positive ideas regarding the human qualities and institutional shape constituting this future order are anti-individualist and expressed in the purest egalitarian idiom. Fanon considers, for example, that the people in colonial lands should not look upon themselves as 'individuals', but as brothers, sisters, friends. In tones reminiscent of Buonarotti, Fanon says: 'The motto "look out for yourself", the atheist's method of salvation, is in this context forbidden.' [6] He is looking towards the peasant masses and the urban 'lumpenproletariat' of colonial lands for the achievement of freedom and the re-conquest of human dignity. In the colonial situation, Fanon argues, it is the poor peasants, and not Marx's industrial proletariat, who compose the revolutionary class; it is they who have nothing to lose and all to gain. In Fanon's opinion the peasants are capable of developing the human qualities necessary for the struggle: '... in their spontaneous movements the country people as a whole remain disciplined and altruistic'. [7] We might note, further, that for Fanon even the lumpenproletariat achieves this revolutionary significance on account of its assumption of the requisite human qualities—in clear and relevant contrast to the Western libertarian lumpenproletariat: 'So the pimps, the hooligans, the unemployed and the petty criminals, urged on from behind, throw themselves into the struggle for liberation like stout working men. These classless idlers will by militant and decisive action discover the path that leads to nationhood.' [8] Fanon died an untimely death and his brand of militant anti-Western socialism has not yet borne fruits in Africa. His writings, however, have greatly contributed to the reawakening of revolutionary consciousness among the Negro population of the United States and the West Indies, as shown in the ideological literature of the various Black Power movements.

Turning now to Asia, here of course egalitarian socialism has not merely established itself, but has become a leading political force in a world-wide context. As we have already remarked in the previous chapter, Lenin and his Bolshevik followers, having noted the revolutionary potentials of the Russian peasantry, turned increasingly towards Asia in expectation of colonial revolutions—the West European proletariat being accorded correspondingly diminishing attention. Asian Marxist leaders like M. N. Roy from India were already in the 1920s arguing in favour of shifting the balance of Comintern politics away from Europe—Lenin himself was not wholly convinced. It was in China, potential great power and subjected to humiliation at the hands of Western countries, that Asian socialism was destined to play soon the dominant role. The Chinese Communist Party, after a protracted period of armed struggle, emerged victorious in 1949, proclaiming the world's most populous People's Republic.

During their fight for ascendancy, the communists built their base in the Chinese countryside. Like Russia, China had no sizeable urban working class. But unlike the Leninists, the Chinese relied not on a small band of professional revolutionaries, but on a guerilla army which succeeded in penetrating and bringing to its side the Chinese peasantry. Their leader, Mao Tse-tung, declared in 1927: 'The poor peasants have always been the main force in the bitter fight in the countryside . . . They are the most responsive to Communist Party leadership.' [9] The Chinese under Mao went further than any other Marxist party in turning Marxist communism into a national ideology and a national force—while retaining the language and adapting the concepts of internationalism. They have always concentrated on the territorial conflict, seeing in Western imperialism their main enemy. Intransigent

Socialism

(though not, on the whole, aggressive) in foreign policy, internally their main effort has been the unification of the whole Chinese people under communist leadership. Thus not only the peasants, but also the petty bourgeoisie and even the progressive wing of the 'national bourgeoisie', were brought into Mao's famous 'Four Class Bloc', the communists being, as an historian has remarked, the spokesmen for the nation's 'general will'.[10]

At the time when Stalinism was being denounced in Russia and European Marxism was turning more resolutely towards rationalism, China sprang ahead, soon claiming to represent the leading force in world communism. After the abortive 'Hundred Flowers Campaign' (an attempt at liberalization), Mao instituted his 'Great Leap Forward' and established productive 'communes'. The Soviet leadership objected to these policies, being jealous of their world hegemony and accusing the Chinese of adventurism. These experiments, to be sure, failed at this time, and a few more years were to pass before Mao was able to take the next step. In the meantime the estrangement between China and the Soviet Union grew ever more pronounced, the Chinese branding the Soviets for their 'revisionist' policies, and the latter, in turn, complaining of the 'spirit of chauvinism' in China and of indoctrination of the masses there with 'China's messianic role' in the world.[11] The Chinese remained steadfast in their acknowledgment of Stalin as an outstanding past leader of world communism—although Stalin had not favoured them in the period of the Chinese Civil War, and, even more importantly, the emerging policies of Mao were basically different from Stalin's.[12] No doubt, Mao's apotheosis by his followers as the greatest Marxist-Leninist thinker and political leader does not merely resemble the Stalinist 'cult of the individual', but goes considerably beyond it; Stalin did not put himself openly above the party and his maxims were not sufficiently quotable (with a few exceptions) to be used in the form of incantations. Stalin's power lay in the party organization; Mao's in direct contact with militant forces in the people.

The most dramatic apogee of Maoism was reached in 1966 with the 'Great Proletarian Cultural Revolution'. In an entirely unprecedented fashion, the Chinese leader encouraged and made common cause with the most militant and idealistic of young cadres (the 'Red Guards') in an effort completely to purge and shake up the party apparatus and assume power in the land. Established state and party functionaries had to leave their posts. The Maoists, aided by the People's Liberation

Army, pitted themselves against forces in the party who were taking the 'capitalist road', that is, adopting rationalist policies. The aim of the Cultural Revolution, as an ongoing process, has been the rejuvenation of militant egalitarian elements in Chinese socialism and the checking of tendencies towards bureaucratization. Constant discussion and debate were to replace hierarchical decision-making processes, active and conscious participation at all levels to complement and fertilize the role of the party and influence its leader. The events in China in 1966–9 at the very least opened up vistas for socialist development which should not be underrated.

Mao's thought, mainly as revealed in his pronouncements in the Cultural Revolution but also in earlier periods, is characterized by Marxist-Leninist orthodoxy as well as dynamic originality, infused with a spirit of ardent idealism. In 1949 he asserted :'As long as there are people, every kind of miracle can be performed under the leadership of the Communist Party.' [13] The policies of the Great Leap as well as the Cultural Revolution could be justified only on the basis of a voluntarist belief in human ability to change objective conditions, which goes even beyond Lenin's. Correspondingly, although retaining Marxist elitism and centralism, Mao has tended always to preserve direct ideological contact with the 'masses' as a method of arriving at correct policies. To take a typical passage from 1943 :

... take the ideas of the masses (scattered and unsystematic ideas) and concentrate them (through study turn them into concentrated and systematic ideas), then go to the masses and propagate and explain these ideas until the masses embrace them as their own, hold fast to them and translate them into action, and test the correctness of these ideas in such action.[14]

Like a red thread, the fighting egalitarian notions of 'discipline', 'service' and selfless devotion run through Mao's writings. He rejects, for example, 'ultra-democracy', the chief source of which is 'the petty bourgeoisie's individualistic aversion to discipline'.[15] Again, in his famous directive on 'combating liberalism', Mao describes one type of liberalism in these terms: 'Not to obey orders but to give pride of place to one's own opinions. To demand special consideration from the organization but to reject its discipline.' [16] Liberalism, he asserts, 'stems from petty bourgeois selfishness, it places personal interest first and the interests of the revolution second.' [17] And: 'At no time and in no circumstances should a Communist place his personal interests first; he should subordinate them to the interests of the nation and of the masses.' [18] Later Mao has declared: '. . . freedom is freedom with leadership and this democracy is democracy under centralized guidance, not anarchy. Anarchy does not accord with the interests or wishes of the people.' [19] The task of building communism, as Mao has seen it, is mainly through education whereby people gain the 'correct political point of view'. Economic construction is to be achieved by diffused will-power and mass mobilization, not by managerial-technological elitism. 'We must spread the idea of building our country through diligence and frugality.' [20] With a relentless drive that has easily surpassed Soviet efforts to abolish the division of labour, the Chinese leader has insisted, especially during the Cultural Revolution period, that intellectuals should take full part in productive work. As he has said: 'We encourage the intellectuals to go among the masses, to go to factories and villages. It is very bad if you never in all your life meet a worker or a peasant.' [21] The whole atmosphere of Maoism is stern, and in some by no means irrelevant respects definitely puritanical; [22] it is shot through with fanatical, unrelenting faith in coming world communism.

We might note here briefly yet another and most interesting feature of Mao's thought, namely his views on 'contradiction'. These, in spite of their terse, classical simplicity, recapture an aspect of Marxism which had been lost both by dogmatic, Soviet-style materialist philosophy and by resurrected neo-Left Hegelian Marxist 'humanism'. It may even be argued that Mao's doctrine of contradition in its consistent dialectical realism surpasses and improves on the original Marxian view itself. His direct statements on the universality of contradiction might not, at first glance, sound too exciting or original: 'Contradiction is universal and absolute, it is present in the process of development of all things and permeates every process from beginning to end' [23]—sentences like this are to be found in all major theoretical writings of Marxist thinkers. However, the point is that Mao actually *means* that contradiction is universal, and most significantly he breaks with the widely accepted Marxian views to the effect that contradiction (e.g. the dialectic) comes to an end in 'communism'. As an inspired editorial in the central organ of the Chinese Communist Party stated in 1956:

> . . . not everybody will be perfect, even when a communist society is established. By then there will still be contradictions

among the people, and there will still be good people and bad, people whose thinking is relatively correct and others whose thinking is relatively incorrect.[24]

The same views are expressed also in one of Mao's most influential tracts, 'On the Correct Handling of Contradictions Among the People', where, for example, it is acknowledged that there are contradictions between the 'people' and the 'government' in China.[25] This decisive break by Maoism with the naïve utopianism inherent in much of Marx's doctrines might in the longer run be seen to be Mao's most important contribution to socialist thought; more important than some aspects of Red Guard activities, misconstrued by many Western New Left commentators as manifestations of libertarianism.

Apart from the points listed above Maoism has achieved worldwide influence also on account of the Chinese teaching on 'people's war', guerilla tactics and armed popular insurrection designed progressively to liberate colonial dependencies, thus encircling the global 'city' of imperialism by occupying the world's 'countryside'. National liberation movements in, for example, South-East Asia and to some extent Palestine have put Maoist teaching to the test of experience. Note, however, that for all its boldness and originality Maoism is still 'Marxist-Leninist' in its upholding of the vanguard communist 'party' as the chief locus of revolutionary ideological and political power. However, events in Latin America succeeded in pushing egalitarian socialism one step further. Here the victory of the Cuban revolution and the pattern of the new society inaugurated on the island have, to all appearances, opened yet another chapter in the unfolding of socialism. Of course, Cuba is not Latin America, and recent experience is too inconclusive to suggest that this pattern could be extended; though the fate of the Allende administration in Chile would not seem to augur well either, from the point of view of the 'constitutional' achievement of socialism in a Latin American context. On the other hand, Latin America is sufficiently 'Latin', in spite of the accretion of North American and other cultural influences, to suggest that the striking revival here of the purest French classical-revolutionary egalitarian traditions would have a more fertile soil than elsewhere in the Third World. A notable and relevant development here has been also the attitude of considerable sections of the Roman Catholic clergy sympathizing with revolutionary socialist forces and often actively fighting established political systems based on cruel oppression, glaring injustices and the servile acceptance of United States economic interests.[26]

The Cuban experiment, though it has many intriguing facets, is relevant to our discussion mainly for two reasons. In the first place, here was an armed insurrection, led by a handful of intellectuals and supported mainly by poor peasants, which succeeded in wrenching Cuba from the Western capitalist world and in establishing a socialist system there which is second to none, including China, in its boldly idealistic egalitarian designs—and all this *without* the active involvement of the orthodox Cuban Communist Party. It is true that Fidel Castro claimed (in 1961, two years after the revolution) always to have been a 'Marxist'. However, the point remains that the Cuban revolution brought to the surface a novel kind of socialist revolutionary process: one that has grown out of armed insurrection, bypassing the hitherto obligatory Marxist ideological preparatory work and political organization—as Régis Debray, the French Marxist writer, described it.[27] While the orthodox communists in Latin America were scheming, Castro and his band of insurrectionists took to arms and conquered. This leads us to the second point. Due no doubt to a large extent to Cuba's relative isolation in the Western hemisphere and the intransigent attitude of the United States and exiled elements of the ancient regime, the Cuban system has from the very beginning been characterized by greater internal militancy, mass mobilization and bold social experimentation than other Marxist systems. The personal background and idealism of the erstwhile guerilla-fighters, now leaders of the Cuban state, have also been important contributory factors. In Debray's words, the guerillas' way of life incarnated true 'proletarian morality', in contrast to the city-dwellers' 'infantile and bourgeois' habits generated in urban surroundings—these 'lukewarm incubators'.[28] One conspicuous result has been the celebrated Cuban method of stimulating production and achieving industrialization by the adoption of 'moral incentives', in stark (though sometimes underemphasized) contrast to the Soviet Stalinist 'Stakhanovite' system whereby production is boosted by heavy individual material bonuses. The method of moral incentives, drawing on the 'communitarian' and 'play-motives' and instituting agricultural 'festivals'[29] (in striking resemblance to Rousseau's egalitarian vision), has by no means achieved complete success; but it has gone far enough to deserve a prominent place in any, even the most superficial, sketch of the Cuban experience.

The chief influence behind the egalitarian drive in Cuba was Ernesto Che Guevara, Castro's plenipotentiary for financial and industrial affairs in the early 1960s. Guevara's worldwide popular appeal stemmed, it is true, primarily from his international activities, notably his participation in guerilla war in Latin America, leading to his death in the Bolivian jungle in October, 1967. A most daring fighter and a willing martyr, Guevara certainly lived out in his person the egalitarian ideal, even though, in his views and actions on the guerilla front, he reached beyond the threshold of reasonable militancy, his position, in the words of a recent commentator, bordering 'on being what communists frequently call adventurism or Blanquism'.[30] A less spectacular but more solid monument to his memory, therefore, will be found in his constructive work in founding Cuba's egalitarian society. An indication of the character of this work can be gleaned from a brief selection of statements Guevara made during his Cuban career.

On the question of incentives in production, Guevara noted that there was an objective need for material stimulants while refusing to accept them as a 'fundamental driving force'. He looked upon material incentive rather as a 'necessary evil', and warned: 'It must not be forgotten that it comes from capitalism and is destined to die under socialism.'[31] Therefore, he regarded it as 'the function of the vanguard party . . . to raise the opposite banner as high as possible—the banner of interest in non-material things. . . .'[32] Above all it would be necessary, he asserted, to inculcate a new attitude to work. For the new consciousness 'work ceases to be the obsession it is in the capitalist world and becomes a pleasant social duty. It is engaged in happily, to the accompaniment of revolutionary songs, amidst fraternal camaraderie and human relationships which are mutually invigorating and uplifting'.[33] But he realized at the same time that socialist construction is an arduous task which cannot always be translated into immediate pleasure. 'Industrialization,' he admitted, 'is built of sacrifices.'[34] And he warned young communists that apart from the 'great spirit of sacrifice' displayed in a revolution, 'there ought to be a spirit of sacrifice not reserved for heroic days only, but for every moment'.[35]

Guevara rejected individualism in the clearest terms possible: 'Individualism, in the form of the individual action of a person alone in a social milieu, must disappear in Cuba. In the future individualism ought to be the efficient utilization of the whole individual for the absolute benefit of a collectivity.'[36] Again: 'Most important is the nation. It is the entire people of Cuba, and you have got to be ready to sacrifice any individual benefit for the common good'.[37] It was his, and of course no less Castro's, view, that 'to build communism a new man must be created simultaneously with the material base',[38] a cadre who is an 'individual of ideological and administrative discipline, who knows and practises democratic centralism', 'a creator, a leader of high stature'.[39] In view of Guevara's posthumous elevation by the Western New Left as a 'symbol', it is instructive to note the following statement for its crystal-clear opposition to fashionable libertarian notions (though as likely as not the egalitarian import of this and similar exhortations by Guevara can be explained away or simply ignored):

> Our vanguard revolutionaries must idealize their love for the people, for the most hallowed causes, and make it one and indivisible. They cannot descend, with small doses of daily affection, to the terrain where ordinary men put their love into practice.[40]

Castro has continued the building of Cuba in the same spirit, endeavouring to create 'socialist society' and 'communist man' at the same time. If anything, his pronouncements on the tasks facing his countrymen and on the society Cuba is erecting tend to be even more harshly egalitarian than Guevara's. In a speech, for instance, Castro said in 1968:

> ... it is clear that capitalism has to be pulled out by the roots. We cannot encourage or even permit selfish attitudes among men if we don't want man to be guided by the instinct of selfishness, of individuality; by the wolf, the beast instinct; man as the enemy of man, the exploiter of man, the setter of snares for other men. . . . The concept of socialism and communism, the concept of a higher society, implies a man devoid of those feelings; a man who has overcome such instincts at any cost; placing, above everything, his sense of solidarity and brotherhood among men.[41]

It was two years after Guevara's demise, in 1969, that Castro declared: '. . . the Revolution aspires—as one of the steps toward communism— to equalize incomes from the bottom up, for all workers, regardless of the type of work they do.' [42] There have been positive measures, such as the successive inclusion of various community services into the freely provided category, as well as the promise to 'abolish the use of money' in the near future. Castro's reaction to the Soviet armed attack on the Dubcek regime sounded a jarring note, embarrassing many socialists in the West, but it was perfectly logical from his standpoint. As he said: 'We are against all those bourgeois liberal reforms within Czechoslovakia . . . as series of reforms that increasingly tended to accentuate mercantile relations within a socialist society: personal gain, profit, all those things.' [43]

Now in turning to evaluation we might well begin by making a few brief remarks on a kind of interpretation and criticism of the Chinese and (especially) the Cuban experience, which, though sympathetic and helpful, also tend to confuse fundamental issues. The error, it seems, stems from mistaking the nature of egalitarianism or from failure to recognize it as an independent, basic tendency of socialism. Two instances will suffice to illustrate the point. Irving Horowitz, in criticizing Debray, notes that for Debray 'the physical symbol of the new Left is the military tunic'; and he asks: 'But is not the physical representation of the old Right also the military tunic?' [44] René Dumont, reporting on the activities in Cuban youth camps, argues that in so far as these prefigure Cuban communism, 'this sort of communism is devilishly close to army life. In that case we are no longer dealing with a future society, for the army is a very old institution that goes back for millennia'.[45] Now the point we are trying to argue is that *some* degree of 'militariness' (after all, 'militant' and 'military' are related concepts) is *necessarily* involved with egalitarian socialism, whether or not it shares this with the 'army' as 'a very old institution'—so is egalitarianism, its roots, in fact, being even older. The notions of service, devotion, selflessness or self-transcendence can only be made sense—intellectual as well as practical—in the framework of a unitary community imbued with an overriding purpose. Thus there are certain things for which it makes no sense to criticize egalitarian societies, such as their austerity, their relative lack of charity, their intolerance, their drabness and poverty, their failure to allow 'public protest' or 'dissent'. Egalitarian ideals command the highest respect; egalitarian practice must always be treated with caution. The price of egalitarianism is sublimated suffering; just as the price of rationalism is materialism and inequality, and that of moralism is weakness and proneness to compromise.

Dumont, who is not merely a sympathetic observer, but knows Cuba intimately, unfortunately *conflates* the above erroneous criticism with perfectly valid and pertinent remarks dealing with Cuba's failure to live up to the egalitarian ideal itself. While 'militariness' should not be maligned, the same is not true of *militarism*, especially if, as Dumont asserts, in the Cuban case it is accompanied by increasing 'petty bourgeois' ascendancy over workers and peasants and by the surreptitious survival of 'material incentives' for higher executives. Other observers also confirm widespread dissatisfaction in Cuba with 'moral incentives' and economic organization.[46] These charges, if true, do not of course concern egalitarianism any longer: their target is emerging Stalinism, in its more or less overt form.

Is, then, egalitarianism inherently unstable? Will it be necessary to start 'cultural revolutions' even in countries like China in every decade or in every generation? Questions and doubts inevitably enter into the observer's mind when surveying the situation. In trying to account for the seeming instability of egalitarianism, however, one ought not to have recourse to metaphysical explanations. There are two prime candidates in this category and their value is questionable. One explanation is in terms of a supposedly eternal 'human nature' containing ineradicable biological or physiological traits which lead to the necessary reproduction of features like inequality, aggression and selfishness in every kind of society. But this fails to take into account the variety of human societies and the fact that, even if for short periods only, significant reductions in inequality combined with heightened group-solidarity and the repression of egoism have already been achieved—in wars and revolutions for example. Another, similar, explanation is in terms of 'development', using the model of Western nations to show that industrialization and high productivity must lead to and/or be accompanied by individualism of one kind or another. But—though there are aspects of this argument which would necessitate a more thorough-going discussion—one might here call attention to the historical *contingency* of the combined development of industrialization-secularization-capitalism in the West, and to the consequent 'underdeveloping' of other parts of the world.[47] So there is no compelling reason to suppose that the Western historical conjuncture would be repeated elsewhere.

There are, in fact, more mundane factors which might illuminate some of the difficulties confronting egalitarian regimes. Firstly, there is the fact that countries, even if they are as large and populous as China, exist and function in a complex network of international relations. There can be no sustained periods of splendid isolation, especially for states which are experimenting with radical innovations in economic and social organization. China in the late sixties was effectively isolated from the rest of the world, except for Albania and 'Marxist-Leninist' splinter groups of communist parties the world over. For a small country like Cuba, again, foreign trade is a vital necessity, and besides the diplomatic obligations imposing certain internal norms, the effects of economic competition on the international level are bound to be disruptive of the internal productive process. It is something like a vicious circle: internally egalitarianism flourishes on the intensification of national feeling and on a sense of danger and isolation (like the egalitarian *kibbutzim* in Israel), but these very same factors make it more difficult for the egalitarian community to co-exist with other states. Or, to put it another way, egalitarian socialism could only become stable on a worldwide basis, but can only take root in a national context, and this in turn prevents or retards its further extension.

This leads to another point. One feature of nationalism, very much in evidence with the socialist regimes we have been discussing, is its tendency to universalization. This is an involuntary, unconscious process: Chinese, Cuban, etc. socialists tend not to notice that their 'socialism', both as blueprint and as an effective principle of organiza-tion, bears on itself indelible marks of particular national traditions.[48] Of course, this is true of Leninism as a whole too: 'communist' party organization everywhere is an extended projection of (Lenin's own interpretation of) Russian experience. However, this pattern may still be more flexible, and hence more amenable to export, than projections based on the Chinese and Latin American traditions. Socialists in the Third World rightly feel uneasy when exhorted, quite innocently, to follow the Chinese or Cuban examples. But again, 'internationaliza-tion' and hence applicability in wider contexts might mean precisely the kind of *dilution* of these and other national models which would effectively neutralize their dynamic egalitarian character.

Lastly, egalitarian regimes are constantly exposed to the rival attrac-tion of rationalist socialism, which, after all, predominates in the most powerful and richest socialist states. While capitalist restoration would not appear to present an immediate peril in either Cuba or China, the example of efficiently run and increasingly prosperous one-party states provides a more congenial and respectable alternative; [49] calling these rationalist regimes 'revisionist' and the like merely highlights the problem, but does not alter the fact.

Still, irrespective of their relative instability, egalitarian regimes and movements in the Third World have understandably acted as a powerful stimulus for socialists in advanced industrial, mainly Western, society. The fanaticism and selfless devotion of the Chinese Maoists and the heroism of the Latin American *guerillero* have conjured up pictures of what European socialism itself might have been. However, in the West the egalitarian tendency encounters its most formidable radical rival, its polar opposite: libertarianism. The latter, in its extant forms, is indigenous to advanced industrial society only. Here radical socialism, as distinguished from desophistication in the Third World, manifests itself through the rise of theory to the giddiest heights. Our last chapter will be devoted to this topic, libertarianism being also the last (in the sense of most recent) phenomenal appearance in the unfolding spirit of socialism.

9 Libertarianism: The Love-Makers

Radical socialism or the 'New Left' in the West has assumed a variety of forms and shapes in recent years. We shall, however, focus our discussion in this chapter primarily on ideas and movements which exemplify the libertarian tendency in operation—and even here the limelight will mainly fall on a rather narrow area. This may at first seem unfair and misleading, not least on account of the fact that libertarianism, after its meteoric appearance and successes in the late 1960s, seems today to have lost some of its popular appeal. Yet our choice—and the element of abstraction and distortion it necessarily inflicts on the whole subject matter—may be justified, on the following grounds. Firstly, libertarianism is peculiar—perhaps unique—to advanced industrial Western society; it constitutes *the* specific radicalism and radical socialism belonging intrinsically to the West; it is Western society's special contribution to contemporary socialist development. Second, it is imperative in our context to turn after egalitarianism to its polar opposite: only by highlighting the *contrast* between the various departures in socialism can we hope to achieve something even faintly resembling a rounded presentation, a picture complete in its outlines.

Libertarianism, then, defines the ideas and attitudes of those whom we call the 'love-makers'. The term seems appropriate (even though somewhat flippant) on two counts. Advocates of libertarian radicalism conceive of the ideal society in terms of 'love', both physical and spiritual. Also, many of them tend to see in 'love' the best method through which to attain this ideal. 'Make love, not war', as the chief libertarian slogan is in a markedly different style, or dimension, from more established mainstream socialist objectives such as 'building peace' or 'achieving the socialist transformation of society'. Libertarianism and its critique of society are essentially inward-looking, emotion-based and individualistic. The emphasis is on immediacy and spontaneity, on the direct display of alternatives, rather than on conventional political struggle. The critique concentrates not so much on social relations as on personal relations and a whole way of life. Here the outstanding issues are not exploitation and inequality, but universal oppression; instead of a ruling class, the enemy is seen in terms of an impersonal 'system' or one's own 'manipulated' consciousness. In Charles Reich's words, 'the enemy is within each of us; so long as that is true, one structure is as bad as another'.[2] The advocates of libertarianism, further, are not the underdogs in the conventional sense, but disaffiliated and rebellious members of the middle and upper class: intellectuals, artists, students, women, sections of the clergy. Neither is it an accident that the dominant social and ideological base of libertarianism should be the United States, the inner fortress of Western advanced capitalism. As we have already noted in Chapter 5, the peculiar situation of the United States has prevented there the growth of socialism in its egalitarian, rationalist and moralist forms. The very same factors, however, have made for the ascendancy of libertarianism: prosperity and abundance as well as the radical individualist tradition in America have made disaffiliated groups, particularly intellectuals and a section of middle-class youth, receptive to modern libertarian ideas. The new Western radical style thus bears the unmistakable imprint of American attitudes on itself.[3]

What made for the emergence of the new libertarian style in the 1960s? Our answer can be no more than tentative, listing a few obvious contributory factors, while not for a moment pretending that the list is exhaustive. On the practical side there appear to be the following principal causes: the nature of advanced capitalist society itself, with its unprecedented general prosperity, relative security, relative welfare, relative freedom of movement, speech and association. The pattern is (or was until quite recently) the uniform, colourless, boring, predictable 'consumer society', with the bulk of the working class securely integrated, and opposition becoming the function of intellectuals and the lumpenproletariat. Secondly on this count we must refer to the experience of the end of the Cold War and the resultant relief from the fear of imminent nuclear catastrophe. These turned critical energies more inward and at the same time loosened existing ideological controls. Thirdly, as we have already noted earlier, there has been a deep and wide (and predictable) disillusionment on the part of the masses in *all* conventional varieties of socialism: social democracy, following the bulk of the working class into social integration, has lost its dynamism; Leninism, as an ideology presupposing deep social cleavages and egalitarian militancy, has failed to come in from the cold.

Before coming to the theoretical sources of libertarianism, we must make one thing clear. It is a myth that the libertarian, love-making New Left is 'anti-intellectual'. On the very contrary, it is hyper-intellectual, over-sophisticated, inescapably avant-garde: its very essence is the Himalaya-jump of theory over plain common consciousness. The 'unity of theory and praxis' of liberated members of the New Left (like the 'Underground') is in stark contrast to both the consciousness and the way of life outside; as opposed to the unity of theory and praxis to be found in the egalitarian socialism of the Third World, here radical theory and libertarian life-style have not arisen from the felt needs and desires of the masses. But we shall come back to this point below.

As regards the theoretical background, then, we ought to distinguish between negative and positive influences. Negatively, mention must be made of the decline in the intellectual prestige of science (of which the plight of 'scientific socialism' is but one manifestation). This decline seems to be a direct consequence of dazzling scientific advances: technology, whether of computers, H-bombs or space research, frightens and overwhelms. Scientific rationality has, consequently, ceased to be seen as the key to progress. Thus we have at the very height of advanced industrial civilization the resurgence of pre-Enlightenment forms of belief and their (amazingly successful) incorporation into radical criticism: witchcraft, astrology, magic. Positively, we ought to make at least a brief reference to the increased impact of oriental religion and philosophy: Zen Buddhism, Hinduism, mysticism, 'mind-expansion' through drugs and contemplation as well as various 'non-violent techniques' of resistance and struggle, have found their way into the radical armoury. Thus, although libertarianism is a Western phenomenon, its sources come also from the East. Another influence has been modern existentialist philosophy, with its pioneering concern with the 'lonely' and 'lost' individual in search of 'authenticity' and 'commitment'.

We must, however, also note the indigenous socialist ideological ingredients of the new style. Just as today's militant egalitarianism relates directly to the egalitarian tendency of old, libertarianism likewise grows out of native traditions. Hence it may be misleading to call even this phenomenon in the New Left 'new': its novelty lies in its recent success in coming to the surface, not in its birth. While the other basic tendencies of socialism have had their public trial, the libertarian strand has had its incubatory period. Under the shadow of Marxism and social democracy it slowly matured, and has now found its natural milieu in advanced industrial society. Libertarianism is, of course, not to be equated with anarchism, but obviously the ideological predominance of the former also signifies a resurgence of anarchism in various—conventional as well as modern—forms.[4] Basically libertarianism is the same tendency as we have encountered in the case of various earlier (and not only expressly anarchist) thinkers, that strain of radical thought which saw man primarily in terms of 'passion', 'emotion' and 'instinct'. It would be pointless (and impossible) to name any particular thinker in the past who could be regarded as the 'father' of modern libertarianism. What we are confronted with is a composite picture to which many have contributed. Libertarianism draws on the young Marx whose notion of 'alienation' has become one of the most frequently encountered (and much abused) terms in the new ideology. However, many people have found that even the young Marx was not sufficient as a source of inspiration, and the search had gone on to anchor libertarianism on to more and more explicitly radical romantic foundations. Not only, as some would allege, has Bakunin had his posthumous revenge on Marx (in the shape of Leninist elitism and putschism); so have, finally, the spirit of Fourier, Stirner and the Marquis de Sade. As distinguished from Marx's rationalist emphasis on the conquest of external nature, and his egalitarian accent on the community, libertarians turn inward, intent on finding man's own innermost nature. Among the several departures in this search, the greatest prominence attaches to the tendency which claims to have found man's true nature in *sexuality*.

It is of paramount importance to see clearly what this change in orientation involves. The liberation of man from sexual restrictions and the acceptance of sexuality as an integral part of human nature have always been among the ultimate objectives of *all* forms of socialism—without exception. There have been, it is true, temporary constraints and individual socialist thinkers with markedly conservative views on sex, but socialist movements have been sexually progressive. (This is true even of Stalinism, *contra* libertarian assertions: it may have been retrograde in comparison with the experience of the first years of the Soviet Union, but certainly progressive in contrast to old Russian society.) Marx and Engels, in particular, were unmistakably clear in their rejection of 'bourgeois morality' on sex and of monogamous marriage as well as the compulsive family. However, it is still true to say, that, apart from a few exceptions, mainstream and influential socialist thinkers did not regard man as *primarily* a sexual being, and consequently did not consider the abolition of sexual restrictions to have first priority. On the contrary, many of them thought that sexuality, while good in itself, has nevertheless to be ordered in the service of 'higher ends'. Thus sexual liberation with a view to enhancing communal consciousness has been the egalitarian perspective on this question. Perhaps we can illuminate the point by quoting two well-known, and oft-cited, socialist leaders. Lenin, in his celebrated conversation with Klara Zetkin, enlarged on his familiar 'glass-of-water' conception of sexuality:

> Surely, thirst demands to be quenched. But will a normal individual, under normal circumstances, lie down in the gutter and drink from a puddle? Or even from a dirty glass? What is more important than everything else is the social side. Drinking water is an individual act. Love requires two people and may result in a third life. This fact contains a social interest, a duty towards society.[5]

Alexandra Kollontai, Lenin's comrade-in-arms, in a very similar vein considered that 'moral norms regulating sexual life' did have legitimate aims. These she saw, like Lenin, to lie in their instrumentality in bringing the egalitarian ideal nearer. Sexual norms, she asserted, were there:

> To develop and refine the human psyche: to develop in the human spirit feelings of comradeship, solidarity and the emotional experience of being part of the collective.[6]

The view that man's basic nature was to be understood in terms of passion, instinct and sexuality, instead of it lying in sociality, labour and the transformation of nature, that is, the inward-looking, individual-centred tendency, was, as we have noted, for a long time in an ideological and political limbo. It gained tremendous impetus, however, through new departures in the science of psychology at the turn of the century. Psychology thus became a serious rival to economics and sociology as the chief scientific pillar of socialism. Here, of course, the central 'Hegel' or 'Ricardo' figure is Sigmund Freud, the founder of psychoanalysis. Freud was by no means a radical or a socialist in his political views, yet he became the chief prophet of the prophets on the New Left. The latter, an impressive bevy of thinkers, developed their theories in conscious reaction to Freud's discoveries, rejecting many of his conclusions while accepting (like the rest of educated opinion in Western society, especially in America) his basic assumptions. What makes Freud's thought relevant to libertarianism is, of course, his view that man is basically a sexual, instinctive being whose 'anti-social' instinctual energy must be both 'sublimated' and 'repressed' in order for civilization to survive. Now (though this is necessarily a gross over-simplification) the libertarian disciples-cum-critics of Freud have accepted the first point while denying the second; that is, they have argued that man's basic sexuality was not intrinsically anti-social, repression as well as sublimation being necessary only in *this* (i.e. oppressive, exploitative, capitalist, class-ridden) civilization. And they have claimed, further, that in the world of the future real human civilization will be the direct expression of liberated sexuality. Marx was thus married to Freud.

Wilhelm Reich, psychoanalyst and onetime member of the German Communist Party, was the first important Freudo-Marxian theorist and precursor of modern libertarianism. Reich saw the immense revolutionary and subversive potential of Freudian conceptions lying beneath the veneer of positivist scientific respectability. He argued, adapting the relevant Freudian concepts, that the 'reality principle' which individuals have to superimpose on their own instinct, the 'pleasure principle', is 'only the principle of our society'. Further: '. . . the reality principle of the capitalist era imposes upon the proletarian a maximum limitation of his needs while appealing to religious values, such as modesty and humility'.[7] Again: 'Sexual oppression serves class rule: ideologically and structurally reproduced in the ruled, sexual oppression represents the most powerful and as yet unrecognized force of oppression in general.'[8] Reich, therefore, thought that sexual liberation, 'Sex-Pol', was an integral part of the Marxist class struggle, and he set out to instruct young people in ways in which they could best overcome their ideological inhibitions and achieve full sexual satisfaction, a preliminary, so Reich considered, to complete human fulfilment. In particular, here striking out on his own, Reich believed that the inability of the oppressed proletarian individual to achieve 'full orgasm' in sexual intercourse was the main factor keeping him socially oppressed. Reich, however, was expelled from the Communist Party, and subsequently he severed his connections with politics, becoming an out-and-out sexual libertarian,[9] spinning out interesting, though somewhat off-beat, biological theories concerning the repression of sexuality. He was, as it were, in the attic, until rediscovered by the New Left (it has been claimed that his writings were chiefly instrumental in raising the revolutionary consciousness of the students at Nanterre).

It is interesting to note here that although Reich is a true libertarian prophet, the arch-sexual revolutionary whose tracts are still in constant demand, his actual views appear in today's libertarian perspective rather timid, restrictive and conservative. In his Marxist phase, for example, Reich believed in the primacy of political revolution. He also thought, somewhat similarly to Lenin and Alexandra Kollontai, that sexual liberation would lead not to chaos, but to a new 'sexual order'.[10] Furthermore, Reich firmly believed in the natural superiority of heterosexuality and genital satisfaction.[11] Today libertarians argue in favour of complete sexual pluralism and claim the equality of all practices. 'Gay Liberation' and the explosion of 'the myth of the vaginal orgasm' certainly make Reich's theories appear somewhat dated.

On a much higher intellectual level, though also with more eclecticism, the thinkers belonging to the so-called 'Frankfurt School' have taken further, and perhaps perfected, the fusion of Marxism and sexual radicalism. Here, of course, one has also to take into account various motifs from classical German idealism, the resurrected interest in the radical implications of Hegelian philosophy (first stated in striking terms in Georg Lukacs's *History and Class Consciousness*), existentialism and phenomenology as well as distinct echoes of Stirner and Nietzsche, which together produced 'critical philosophy', the intellectual achievement of the School. Its adherents—Horkheimer, Adorno, Fromm, Benjamin and more recently Habermas and Alfred Schmidt—distinguished themselves by putting forward a great variety of influential theories concerning advanced industrial society and its maladies, for example, the theory of the 'authoritarian personality' which was designed to explain fascism and social conformity in general. It is interesting to note that although the Frankfurt School thinkers have been generally looked upon as Marxists (also by themselves), they themselves in fact started the process of gnawing away at the Marxian foundations from a libertarian point of view. Both Horkheimer and Adorno, for example, became highly critical of Marx's concept of labour, which they regarded as the source of an 'ascetic ideology' which would turn the whole world into a 'gigantic workhouse'. Horkheimer, castigating revolutionaries who had adopted the 'hostility to happiness', like Cola di Rienzi, Savonarola and Robespierre, declared his preference for thinkers like Helvetius, de Sade and Nietzsche, the apostles of individualist hedonism.[12]

In the thought of Herbert Marcuse the libertarian critical philosophy of the School succeeded in moving out of the seminar-room into the open spaces of the New Left. Marcuse achieved his fame and influence through his synthesis of critical philosophy and a topical, biting, forceful denunciation of advanced industrial society, the latter stemming from the American tradition of radical sociology. Marcuse asserted, provoking bitter attacks by orthodox Marxists as well as by defenders of the status quo, that in advanced industrial society, under the reign of 'technological rationality', the working class had ceased to be revolutionary in its aspirations, and that the system had managed to absorb, integrate and thus neutralize all criticism. Life and consciousness have become, according to him, 'one-dimensional'. The system's 'supreme promise is an ever-more-comfortable life for an ever-growing number of people who, in a strict sense, cannot imagine a qualitatively different universe of discourse and action'.[13] But, although the system thus 'delivers the goods', generating a kind of superficial, ersatz, manipulated satisfaction, it depends for its very existence on brutal oppression of minorities and on constant war-readiness. Yet today, Marcuse argues, with our highly advanced technology, we could almost immediately move from the phase of the struggle for existence to the 'pacification of existence'. In *Eros and Civilization* Marcuse paints an extravagant, but not unattractive, picture of the future:

> No longer used as a full-time instrument of labour, the body would be resexualized. The body in its entirety would become an object of cathexis, a thing to be enjoyed—an instrument of pleasure . . . from sexuality constrained under genital supremacy to erotization of the entire personality.[14]

To achieve this ideal, he asserts, it is necessary to generate now 'a type of man who is biologically incapable of fighting wars and creating suffering',[15] '. . . men who have developed an instinctual barrier against cruelty, brutality, ugliness'.[16] His vast erudition and overall Marxian perspective, however, have prevented Marcuse from arguing unequivocally in favour of immediate, inner, spontaneous individual 'liberation' which is the hall-mark of libertarianism.[17] Other leading contemporary radicals have had far fewer inhibitions. Writers like

Norman O. Brown, Theodore Roszak, Timothy Leary and Charles Reich in the United States, or R. D. Laing and David Cooper in Britain, have asserted much more forcefully and consistently the primacy of sexual and psychological revolution, their main targets being personal relationships in advanced society, with special reference to the institution of the family.

Here we should refer briefly also to radical feminism, or the Women's Liberation Movement, which seems to constitute the most durable survival from the wave of libertarianism in the 1960s. Now similarly to sexual liberation in general, feminism has always been closely related to socialism (from at any rate the time the latter took over from liberalism as the foremost radical ideology). Again, although some individual writers had markedly conservative opinions on this subject (Rousseau, Proudhon and Belfort Bax are the most obvious examples), socialist *movements* have invariably regarded the emancipation of women as one of their chief aims. Seminal thinkers like Thompson, Marx, Engels and Bebel wrote eloquently on women's equality, while there is a long and impressive line of women, the likes of Flora Tristan, Klara Zetkin, Emma Goldman, Alexandra Kollontai and Rosa Luxemburg, who became outstanding socialist leaders.

But here we come up against an intriguing problem. The political and social emancipation of women is one thing. Complete psychological emancipation, leading to the elimination of conventional 'sex-roles' and qualities, is quite another. Socialism in general, and egalitarianism in particular, have been able to embrace the former; they may not be easily (or at all) reconcilable with the latter. It is, of course, not altogether certain if secondary sexual qualities, putative 'masculine' and 'feminine' characteristics, ought to come into our analysis of socialism at all; our basic tendencies, to be sure, cut across many of these distinctions. However, it is a fact that the prevailing libertarian current in feminism quite deliberately sets out to oppose what it regards as the 'masculine' bias in certain varieties of socialism. Its values and ideological line consciously express what ought properly to be called 'femininism'—as distinguished from 'feminism'. Socialism, certainly as regards the egalitarian and rationalist varieties, is not 'anti-woman' or 'anti-feminist'—but it may well turn out to be incompatible with the libertarian, femininist tendency.

Libertarian advocates of Women's Liberation demand the end of 'patriarchy'. Kate Millett, for example, a hard-line radical writer, regards patriarchy or 'sexual dominion' 'as perhaps the most pervasive ideology of our culture' which 'provides its most fundamental concept of power'.[18] She declares as her aim a 'fully realized sexual revolution' which 'would be a permissive single standard of sexual freedom, and one uncorrupted by the crass and exploitative economic bases of traditional sexual alliances'.[19] This would entail the complete abolition of the family and of sex-roles, and the collectivization of the care of the young. She laments the fact that in the Soviet Union, after a good start, there was a sexual 'counter-revolution', and, going beyond Stalinism, she squarely puts the blame on Marxism itself: 'A still deeper cause is the fact that beyond declaring that the compulsive family must go, Marxist theory had failed to supply a sufficient ideological base for a sexual revolution, and was remarkably naïve as to the historical and psychological strength of patriarchy.'[20] And, significantly, she finds reason for optimism in the fact that today's Western radicalism is libertarian and feminine-oriented, noting 'the revolt of youth against the masculine tradition of war and virility'.[21]

Both Millett and Germaine Greer, another leading libertarian writer, consider that since women constitute the 'largest alienated element' in advanced society, they could and ought to play a 'leadership part' in the coming revolution. According to Greer, women 'are the only true proletariat left, and they are by a tiny margin the majority of the population, so what's stopping them?'[22] She argues that the arrival of socialism is dependent upon the complete achievement of sexual liberation: 'Women's liberation, if it abolishes the patriarchal family, will abolish a necessary substructure of the authoritarian state, and once that withers away Marx will have come true willy-nilly, so let's get on with it'[23] (although she is of the opinion that there is 'more hope for women in Marcuse than in Marx').[24] And she turns resolutely against the traditional egalitarian attitude to revolution: 'Women who adopt the attitudes of war in their search for liberation condemn themselves to acting out the last perversion of dehumanized manhood, which has only one foreseeable outcome, the specifically masculine end of suicide.'[25] Instead of adopting 'male kinds of grouping and organizational structure',[26] women should condemn violence: 'It would be genuine revolution if women would suddenly stop loving the victors in violent encounters'.[27] She asserts, in characteristic libertarian fashion, that 'the end cannot justify the means', and that 'the struggle which is not joyous is the wrong struggle'.[28] In her bestseller, *The Female Eunuch*, we find one of the most explicit manifestoes of libertarianism:

The chief means of liberating women is replacing of compulsiveness and compulsion by the pleasure principle.

The essence of pleasure is spontaneity. In these cases spontaneity means rejecting the norm, the standard that one must live up to, and establishing a self-regulating principle.[29]

A very relevant and interesting point to note here is the theoretically superior—though at the same time often ambivalent and heterogeneous—position taken by Marxist feminist writers. Although evidently affected by the prevailing libertarian style, they strike a more sober and sophisticated note. Juliet Mitchell, for example, in her recent masterly study of Freud shows scepticism towards the libertarian ideal of a 'natural feminized culture', criticizing the vision of a 'primitive matriarchy', 'the reign of nurturing, emotionality and non-repression'. [33] In a more concrete vein, Sheila Rowbotham clearly recognizes the difficulties involved with the synthesizing of the class and sexual struggles: 'The liberation of women has never been fully realized, and the revolution within the revolution remains unresolved. The connection between feminism, the assertion of the claims of women as a group, and revolutionary socialism is still awkward.' [31] She perceives, furthermore, more acutely than many observers (Marcuse for instance) the dimensional difference obtaining between the egalitarian socialist struggle going on in the Third World and the prevalent mode in the West. Of Vietnam, for example, she remarks:

> ... it is not possible to see yet whether the ethic of abstinence and fidelity will survive after the war. As it is it is obviously an integral part of the military morale, and provides a needed contrast to the degradation of the brothels for the U.S. troops in the South. In this context ideas of sexual liberation are somehow incongruous.[32]

We might suggest, of course, that this observed discrepancy between East and West involves more than a difference of 'context'. It may be seen as a concrete manifestation of the basic divide between the two polar tendencies of socialism, which, while mutually complementary at certain junctures, yet pull in opposite directions. The spectacular successes of the New Left in the 1960s, the series of 'confrontations' all over the world, the American draft-resistance campaign, the occupation of university campuses, the West German extra-parliamentary opposition, and last but not least the 1968 eruption in France, were occasioned by the unique, ephemeral and historically contingent convergence of the two tendencies, with libertarianism preparing the minds and egalitarianism coming to inform the action. Non-violence, flower-power, the demonstrations of life-style, as many observers noted at the time, were soon giving way to the older, and more directly political, forms of struggle. But even at the best of times, the convergence was *felt* by many activists to be precarious. To turn to Sheila Rowbotham again, who has described her experience at the famous conference on the 'Dialectics of Liberation' thus:

> It was a peculiar collection of the incompatible and reluctant forces of liberation. The revolutionary left—or bits of it—encountered the mind-blowers. Having carried them both around inside me for some time I was anxious to see how they would meet. It was more of a two-week long trauma than a conference. I experienced a severe sense of dislocation throughout.[33]

From a rather different standpoint the same recognition is voiced by Richard Neville, commenting on the 'opposing instinct within the Movement which causes so much conflict. The sober, violent, puritan, Left extremists, versus the laughing, loving, lazy, fun-powder plotters'.[34] Though libertarian revolutionaries often show admiration for Maoism or Castroism, their basic attitude to change points to a different dimension altogether. Let alone the advocacy of 'moral incentives', there is every incentive in the libertarian perspective not to accept morality at all. The Cohn-Bendit brothers' view that the task is 'to rid ourselves, in practice, of the Judeo-Christian ethic, with its call for renunciation and sacrifice',[35] is the authentic voice of libertarianism, and it ill accords with subsequent sober Marxist analyses of the Paris events in 1968. As Neville remarks, with pardonable exaggeration, 'the ghost of Trotsky may have been parading the banks of the Seine, but he was stoned'.[36] Others have talked about the chasm between the 'warm' and 'cold' currents in the New Left, the gap between 'play' and 'ritual', the difference between the free-living 'communes' and the neo-Leninist 'red monasteries'.[37] In America Guevara has been turned into a sex-symbol;[38] here a visiting British journalist reported in 1970:

> ... it seems to be assumed that one drawing or photo of the genital organs is equivalent in the revolutionary struggle to two articles exposing the CIA or three editorials denouncing the military-

industrial complex. Nudity is subversive, perversions are defiantly un-American activities, the Red Flag flies from every erection.[39]

Alongside the political relevance of sexuality, drug-taking has also been widely regarded by libertarians as a direct means to revolution. Timothy Leary, for example, connects the basic sex-oriented philosophy of libertarianism with 'mind-expansion'. He believes that 'the crucial variable in today's political equation is age. The basic areas which now divide men are hormonal.'[40] And: 'The overground establishment today just can't see what's happening, can't accept the dedicated, enduring, inevitable existence of the underground . . . The soft chuckle, which comes from neither the left nor the right but some centre within.'[41] And optimistically: 'In twenty years every social institution will have been transformed by the new insights provided by consciousness-expanding experiences.'[42] Or note Neville's view on the contribution of marijuana to the development of the 'new man': '[Marijuana] teaches us to relax again, drains competitive zeal and encourages laziness—which is going to be important in the future.' 'It turns men into stoned Houdinis, who can escape the straitjacket of Aristotelian logic. Lateral thinking, mystical drifters rarely maim other people.'[43]

We may now perhaps venture a few remarks in evaluation of the libertarian tendency. In the first place, there can be no doubt that in theoretical terms libertarianism is more progressive, more daring, more forward-looking than anything else we have encountered in our survey of socialism so far. But there is a glaring, deceptively simple, blindingly obvious fact which should not be blurred by one's intoxication with libertarian theory, namely the fact that this heady theorizing is taking place in an enormous, yawning practical vacuum. It may, furthermore, be argued that the intellectual avant-gardism of libertarian theory is a *direct* consequence of socialism having been unable to achieve more than marginal successes in Western advanced society. The masses are left far behind, occasionally even antagonized with intent, while the liberated consciousness of a radical minority races ahead. This is especially true of the United States, where the 'silent majority' of workers and the lower middle class—both in the rural Bible-belt and in suburbia—stand in growing and bewildered opposition to the ideas and life-style of the hippie counter-culture. Perhaps Marx's view of the Germans, that they transformed into metaphysics the actual political experience of West European peoples, can be adapted to characterize libertarianism in Western advanced industrial society. It is, in other words, only a little bit of an exaggeration to say that libertarianism amounts to a gigantic act of intellectual masturbation, the fantastic transference and sublimation of protracted political impotence. The analogy of masturbation is, of course, doubly relevant here: the elevation of sexuality into the basic principle of human nature leads logically to the acceptance of masturbation as the practice providing the most complete fulfilment. According to recent findings by an American psychologist, the 'perfect orgasm' is the self-administered one; so masturbation is the 'ultimate solution' of sexual liberation.[44] The end of this revolution then is the apothesis of the individual. The 'community' finally fades from the horizon, becomes entirely meaningless.

But this is not much more, after all, than a rhetorical point. A more relevant question is to ask whether or not libertarianism—as here presented—is still a part of, or tendency within, 'socialism'. The answer is by no means an easy one. In one sense, it certainly belongs to socialism: advocates of the sexual or mind-expanding revolution oppose the existing advanced capitalist system, and their values do not appear very different from those cherished by many a socialist 'founding father' in the past. Their methods also, though containing novel aspects, have close resemblance to some traditional forms of protest. They themselves, of course, claim that conventional socialist goals are inadequate, and that existing socialist systems, notably those in the Soviet Union and Eastern Europe, but also in China and Cuba, are 'primitive' or 'arrested' or 'counter-revolutionary' or 'have taken a wrong turn'. Now we have already argued that there is no good reason why either of these varieties (or social democracy) should be denied the socialist label. Prima facie, the same ought to be said about Western libertarianism, as long, of course, as we recognize the features of the particular tendency *it* articulates. And there is another important reason why one should be chary of withholding the socialist label. Its denial to libertarianism would have some unwelcome implications, concealing the admission that socialism in the advanced West has lost much of its former initiative. In the 1960s, at any rate, libertarianism looked all but completely triumphant. If characteristic libertarian pursuits, like dropping-out or bra-burning, are simply labelled 'bourgeois anarchism', then socialism appears rather weak and vulnerable in the West, having to some extent surrendered itself not merely to bourgeois society, but even more embarrassingly to the specific *radicalism* of bourgeois society. Libertarians often claim, with some justice, that their style is in the process of successfully replacing conventional socialist militancy.[45]

But then, if one concedes that libertarianism is a part or aspect of radical socialism in the West, the question still to be asked relates to its effectiveness and viability. What kind of changes can it bring about? For the moment, of course, we are dealing with libertarianism in isolation, viewing it at its purest and most extreme. One thing we can point out with some assurance here. This is that the widely accepted libertarian belief that capitalist society can be overthrown by slowly digging away at its supposed moral and ideological foundations, by attacking the system's soft underbelly, has been shown to be an unwarranted one. Full frontal revelation somehow still does not equal full frontal attack. Advanced industrial society has considerable powers of elasticity and flexibility, and there is overwhelming evidence to show that it is eminently capable of absorbing, and turning to its own advantage, the most daring libertarian innovations and practices. Many writers on the New Left, like Herbert Marcuse in America, Reimut Reiche in West Germany and Sheila Rowbotham in Britain,[46] have noted with clarity this process of absorption and integration, the 'repressive desublimation' (in Marcusean terms) of sexuality and instinctual gratification within the confines of capitalist society. It appears then unlikely that libertarianism could or would lead to full-scale social and political transformation, to something recognizable as an egalitarian revolution. As the playwright Trevor Griffiths has given vent to his frustration in the course of a recent interview: 'I'm fairly convinced that if there's going to be a change here which involves insurrection, it's going to be led by people like Lenin, people prepared to sacrifice their private lives to public needs. I can't see a fun-loving crowd on their third joint taking over the army.'[47]

However, as we have already argued in relation to social democracy, it is also a reductionist mistake to look upon a full-scale egalitarian revolution as constituting the *only* kind of socialism. Love-making libertarianism does find a niche in advanced industrial society; its exploits do represent successes in libertarian terms. These—who can say with certainty?—might point to the kind of socialist development which has the best chance of survival in the present Western situation. The famous 'Provos' and 'Kabouters' of Amsterdam, according to the Dutch anarchist Rudolf de Jong, have taken to selling unfertilized fruit and vegetables in public markets, and have made themselves useful by removing dangerous stones from children's playgrounds. There is thus a fulfilment in community service, in filling the gaps left by the modern Western Welfare State. Furthermore, if you are really intent on 'doing your own thing', you are able to do so; the prevailing system can well afford the 'internal emigration' of a dissenting minority. These and similar pursuits may then appear 'harmless' from a certain point of view, but they are not meaningless. Libertarianism issues in a kind of moralism within the moralism, a contemporary and forceful expression of voluntary charity. In a way it amounts to no more than, in the words of the East German Marxist Wolfgang Harich, the fitting of capitalism with 'new internal decoration' in places 'missed out by the social democratic outfitters'; [48] yet even this is not without significance. The libertarian vision may not command much respect, but, in contrast to egalitarianism, its practice does not give rise to much anxiety either. In comparison to the price to be paid for rationalist or egalitarian socialism, here there is virtually no expenditure involved.

It would be wrong, however, to end our survey on this subdued note. While we cannot take leave with a grand 'conclusion', we can summarily indicate some developments in a wider field not touched upon in the foregoing. The history of socialism, ideas as well as movements, does not come to an end with libertarianism in the West. When it assumes *predominance*, the libertarian tendency reduces the content of socialism. As a fertilizing agency, however, it has led to fruitful progress in several directions. In a fascinating manner, most recent advances in socialist thinking and practice have taken the form of in part *incorporating* libertarianism and in part *reacting* to it. In the theoretical field one need go no further than observing the rebirth of Marx-scholarship, instanced above all by the great interest shown towards Gramsci's theories of cultural hegemony and the role of intellectuals, by the endeavour to connect Marxism to structuralism, by recent work in political economy and in the theory of development. Although, as we have remarked in Chapter 4, these studies have not yet borne practical fruit, they certainly possess a great deal of intrinsic interest.

In the practical field, finally, we may note such areas as trade union militancy and workers' control where, it seems, the influence of anarchist and syndicalist attitudes have resulted in the weakening of large-scale organizational bureaucracy. The widespread tendency towards decentralization and devolution (not confined to socialism, of course), seen in the spontaneous formation of small local communities often inspired by religious fundamentalism, is also, as we have already noted, the result of anarchist and libertarian influences. At this point libertarianism, considerably diluted, can come also to the aid of egalitarian development, though not of the conventional type. The latter is by no means extinct either: it is active in the armed struggle of national or racial minorities for independence, in continuing belligerence (with its heroic as well as cruel and repellent aspects) on the urban front. And so the story goes on.

Notes

1. *What is Socialism?*

1. Cf. '... I am myself a Communist of the old school ... reddest also of the red ... we communists of the old school think that our property belongs to everybody, and everybody's property to us ...' (John Ruskin, *Fors Clavigera*, London, 1896; Vol. I, Letter VII, 'Charities', p. 126). On the other hand, 'socialism' Ruskin associated with republicanism, rationalism and democracy, views which he repudiated. See Quentin Bell, *Ruskin*, London, 1963, p. 49.

2. Hyndman wrote thus in the 'Social Democrat', August 1897, commenting on the proposed unification of his own Social Democratic Federation and the Independent Labour Party. See C. Tsuzuki, *H. M. Hyndman and British Socialism*, Oxford, 1961, p. 102. For leaders of the I.L.P., of course, even the name 'socialist' sounded too militant and revolutionary.

3. See K. Marx, *Die Frühschriften*, Stuttgart, 1932; I, p. 448. Cf. D. McLellan, *The Young Hegelians and Karl Marx*, London, 1969, p. 37.

4. As Engels writes in his 1888 Preface to the English edition, the *Manifesto* is 'undoubtedly the most widespread, the most international production of all socialist literature . . .' (reprinted in K. Marx and F. Engels, *Communist Manifesto*, Moscow, n.d.).

5. As Schumpeter remarked, in connection with Bolshevism, 'the difference of principle has never been fundamental—what there is of it is no less pronounced within the socialist camp than it is as between it and the communist one. Bolsheviks call themselves communists and at the same time the true and only socialists. Whether or not the true and only ones, they are certainly socialists.' (*Capitalism, Socialism and Democracy*, London and New York, 1943, p. 168.) Cf. also the statement: '... everything which gives unity to socialist thought and argument ... is related to the ultimate establishment of what Marx writes about as communism.' (Henry Smith, *The Economics of Socialism Reconsidered*, Oxford, 1962, p. 11.)

6. It would no doubt be presumptuous to call our approach 'dialectical', though it carries the influence of such works as Hegel's *Phenomenology* and some methodological hints found in Marx and Engels as well as more recent Marxist writers. On a more concrete level, inspiration came from W. H. Greenleaf's *The World of Politics* (Inaugural Lecture, Swansea, 1968) and his 'The Character of Modern British Conservatism' (in Robert Benewick, R. N. Berki and Bhikhu Parekh (eds), *Knowledge and Belief in Politics: the Problem of Ideology*, London and New York, 1973, pp. 177–212). As opposed to Greenleaf, however, we would argue that this approach needs no philosophical support from the Wittgensteinian theory of 'family resemblances'; in fact, the latter looks more like a prop to what is in this chapter termed the 'hardheaded' approach. Among works on socialism, Alexander Gray in his most readable but unfortunately rather tendentious and one-sided essay (*The Socialist Tradition: Moses to Lenin*, London, 1946; New York, 1968), makes use of oppositions, such as justice-efficiency and freedom-order (p. 443). Cf. also Henry Smith voicing his opinion on the near-incompatibility between the essential conditions of realizing socialism: '. . . the type of mind that likes simple pleasures is seldom at home in efficient mass-production plants.' (op. cit., p. 210.) In substantive terms, however, we have been chiefly inspired by that brilliant analysis, Emile Durkheim, *Socialism and Saint-Simon* (1928), trans. by C. Sattler, Kent, Ohio, 1958; London 1959. To this work we shall refer again in Chapter 3.

7. Edward Bellamy, *Looking Backward*, London, 1889 (Postscript), p. 192.

2. *The Four Basic Tendencies of Socialism*

1. The nineteenth-century liberal historian, Fustel de Coulanges, accused the moderns of wrongly understanding the ancient world: 'Having imperfectly observed the institutions of the ancient city, men have dreamed of reviving them among us. They have deceived themselves about the liberty of the ancients, and on this very account liberty among the moderns has been put in peril.' And he argues: 'The ancients, especially the Greeks, always exaggerated the importance, and above all, the rights of society; this was largely due, doubtless, to the sacred and religious character with which society was clothed in the beginning.' (*The Ancient City* (1864), Eng. trans., New York, 1963, p. 11, p. 223.) The suggestion we are making, of course, is that the egalitarian tendency in socialism issues precisely out of *this* understanding of the ancient city, seeing true freedom in membership of the community.

2. While it is customary to mention Plato in connection with socialism (on account of his 'communist' elite, the guardians, in *The Republic*), Plato's great successor, Aristotle, seldom gets a reference. Yet it was Aristotle

who, while being severely critical of Platonic 'Communism', identified the fact which is central to the egalitarian tendency, viz. the division of the citizen body into the two fundamental categories of 'rich' and 'poor'. It is this fact which explains the vital distinction between 'democracy' and 'oligarchy'. As he puts it: 'Wherever men rule by virtue of their wealth, be they few or many, there you have oligarchy; and where the poor rule, there you have democracy. But it so happens, as I have said, that the rich are few and the poor numerous.' (*Politics*, London, Everyman, 1959; Book III, p. 79.)

3. Among the countless biblical and patristic pronouncements linking Christianity to socialism we select one, not the most well-known, but the most relevant here (from St Paul's Letter to the Philippians): 'You must never act in a spirit of factiousness, or of ambition; each of you must have the humility to think others better men than himself, and study the welfare of others, not his own.' The very basis of Christianity, the belief in the sacredness of life and immortality of the individual soul, went into the making of the modern consciousness (and moralistic socialism) with only surface alterations. As Hannah Arendt remarks, the modern world 'never even thought of challenging this fundamental reversal which Christianity had brought into the dying ancient world'. (*The Human Condition*, Chicago, 1958, p. 318.)

4. In the golden words of Raphael Hythlodaeus: 'What brand of justice is it that any nobleman whatsoever or goldsmith-banker or moneylender or, in fact, anyone else from among those who either do not work at all or whose work is of a kind not very essential to the commonwealth, should attain a life of luxury and grandeur on the basis of his idleness or his non-essential work? In the meantime, the common labourer, the carter, the carpenter, and the farmer perform work so hard and continuous that beasts of burden could scarcely endure it and work so essential that no commonwealth could last even one year without it. Yet they earn such scanty fare and lead such a miserable life that the condition of beasts of burden might seem far preferable.' (Thomas More, *The Best State of a Commonwealth and the New Island of Utopia*, in *Complete Works*, Vol. 4, New Haven, Conn., 1965, p. 239.) The *Utopia* was written around 1516, when modern society had hardly left its infancy.

5. George Orwell noted disapprovingly 'the prevalence of cranks wherever Socialists are gathered together. One sometimes gets the impression that the mere words "socialism" and "communism" draw towards them with magnetic force every fruitjuice drinker, nudist, sandal-wearer, sexmaniac, Quaker, "Nature Cure" quack, pacifist and feminist in England' (*The Road to Wigan Pier* (1937), Harmondsworth, 1962, p. 152; New York, 1972).

3. *The Emergence of Socialism*

1. The atheist Baron d'Holbach wrote in *La Politique naturelle*: 'Never let us exclaim against inequality, which was always necessary, and is the indispensable condition of our happiness.' (Quoted in Paul Hazard, *European Thought in the 18th Century*, London and Gloucester, Mass., 1965, p. 195.) And Voltaire wrote in his *Philosophical Dictionary*: 'It is impossible in our wretched globe for men living in society not to be divided into two classes . . .' (ed. and trans. by T. Besterman, Harmondsworth and Gloucester, Mass., 1971, p. 182). Cf. also Peter Gay: 'Seeking to distinguish themselves, the philosophes had little desire to level all distinctions; seeking to be respected, they had no intention of destroying respectability.' (*The Enlightenment: An Interpretation*, New York, 1966, and London, 1967; Vol. I, p. 26.)

2. J.-J. Rousseau, *The Social Contract and Discourses*, trans. and introduced by G. D. H. Cole, London (Everyman's University Library), 1973, p. 175 (Everyman's Library, p. 13).

3. ibid., p. 15.

4. In the *Social Contract* Rousseau's demand is merely that 'in respect of riches, no citizen shall ever be wealthy enough to buy another, and none poor enough to be forced to sell himself.' (ibid. p. 42.) But in the less well-known *Constitutional Project for Corsica* he strikes a more modern note: 'Far from wanting the state to be poor, I should like, on the contrary, for it to own everything, and for each individual to share in the common property only in proportion to his services.' (J.-J. Rousseau, *Political Writings*, trans. and ed. by Frederick Watkins, New York, 1953, p. 317.)

5. See R. B. Rose, *The Enragés: socialists of the French Revolution?*, Sydney, 1965.

6. J. L. Talmon, *The Origins of Totalitarian Democracy*, New York, 1961 and London, 1970, p. 150. Talmon's study was epoch-making, and although he overemphasizes the historical links between Rousseau, Jacobinism and Babouvism, and mars his approach otherwise by an abstract, pejorative presentation of 'totalitarian democracy' (which is somewhat similar to our 'egalitarianism'), his analysis is most stimulating. As an antidote, however, see the critique of Talmon in Joan MacDonald, *Rousseau and the French Revolution 1762–1791*, London, 1965.

7. J. L. Carr, *Robespierre: the force of circumstance*, London, 1972, p. 146.

8. In *The Defense of Gracchus Babeuf before The High Court of Vendome*, ed. and trans. by J. A. Scott, Amhurst, Mass., 1967, p. 92.

9. ibid., p. 94.

10. ibid., p. 57.

11. ibid., p. 46.

12. Philippe Buonarotti, *Babeuf's Conspiracy for Equality*, trans. by Bronterre O'Brien, London, 1836, and Clifton, N.J., 1970, p. 155. It is true that the Babouvists reached communism from the angle of 'consumption', being chiefly interested in absolute equality. It seems, however, that Babeuf was moving in the direction of communism of production, too, as shown in a letter of his from prison: 'Will industry perish, because it will no more be exposed to proceed blindly, to take risky adventures, to err by fortuitousness or over-production? Will it go under, because it will be intelligently directed and stimulated in accordance with the needs and well-being of all?' Quoted in Talmon (op. cit.), p. 193.

13. ibid., p. 183.

14. ibid., p. 203.

15. ibid., p. 205.

16. *Defense* (op. cit.), p. 35.

17. See the stimulating historical account in W. J. Fishman, *The Insurrectionists*, London and New York, 1970.

18. Henri Comte de Saint-Simon, *Selected Writings*, ed. and trans. with an introduction by F. M. H. Markham, Oxford and Gloucester, Mass., 1952, p. 8.

19. ibid., p. 47.

20. F. E. Manuel, *The New World of Henri Saint-Simon*, Cambridge, Mass., 1956, p. 237.

21. Saint-Simon (op. cit.), p. 69.

22. ibid., p. 70.

23. ibid., p. 105.

24. Durkheim (op. cit.), p. 196.

25. ibid., p. 141.

26. ibid., p. 52.

27. ibid., p. 71.

28. ibid., pp. 55–6.

29. E. P. Thompson, *The Making of the English Working Class*, Harmondsworth and New York, 1968, p. 859.

30. ibid., p. 863.

31. The reader should compare and contrast the tone, premises and arguments of Owen's *New View* (1814) and his *Report to the County of Lanark* (1821), conveniently reprinted together in Everyman's Library, 1972; also Harmondsworth and Gloucester, Mass., 1969. See also

J. F. C. Harrison, *Robert Owen and the Owenites in Britain and America: The Quest for the New Moral World*, London and New York, 1969, pp. 45–87.

32. Owen believed that productive power 'is already sufficient to saturate the world with wealth, and that the power of creating wealth may be made to advance perpetually in an accelerating ratio.' (*Report*, ibid., p. 202.)

33. See R. K. P. Pankhurst, *The Saint-Simonians, Mill and Carlyle. A Preface to Modern Thought*, London, 1957, p. 15.

34. Mark Hovell, *The Chartist Movement*, London and Clifton, N.J., 1925, p. 33.

35. See John Saville, 'Primitive Accumulation and Early Industrialization in Britain', 'Socialist Register', 1969, pp. 247–71.

36. Charles Hall, *The Effects of Civilization on the People in European States*, London, 1805 and Clifton, N.J., pp. 77–8.

37. William Thompson, *Labour Rewarded. The Claims of Labour and Capital Conciliated . . . etc.*, London, 1827, and New York, 1971, p. 9.

38. William Thompson, *An Inquiry into the Principles of the Distribution of Wealth most conducive to human happiness . . . etc.*, London, 1824, and New York, 1968, p. 381.

39. *The Utopian Vision of Charles Fourier. Selected Texts on Work, Love and Passionate Attraction*, trans. and introduced by J. Beecher and R. Bienvenu, London, 1972, and Boston, Mass., 1971, p. 68. See also J. Carroll, *Break-Out From the Crystal Palace*, London, 1974; an historical account of what the author calls the 'anarcho-psychological tradition' (a main tributary to our 'libertarianism'), acknowledging Fourier to be one of its earliest representatives.

40. ibid., p. 333.

41. George Lichtheim, *The Origins of Socialism*, London, 1968, and New York, 1969, p. 72.

42. See the recent study by Marshall Berman (*The Politics of Authenticity: Radical Individualism and the Emergence of Modern Society*, New York, 1970, and London, 1971), where Rousseau is presented as the founder of 'radical individualism' (i.e. libertarianism). The author, however, accepts willy-nilly in his conclusion that Rousseau moved away from this position and preached later 'totalitarianism' (i.e. egalitarianism).

4. *The Nature of the Marxian Achievement*

1. Leslie Derfler, *Socialism since Marx*, London and New York, 1973; Robert Kilroy-Silk, *Socialism since Marx*, London and New York, 1972.

2. K. Marx, *Economic and Philosophic Manuscripts of 1844*, Moscow, 1961, p. 81.

3. ibid., p. 69.

4. Lewis Feuer, in a stimulating article ('What is alienation? The career of a concept', *New Politics*, I, No. 3, Spring, 1962), points out the romantic origins of the notion of 'alienation': 'The fact of the matter is that "alienation" as first used by Marx, Engels and their fellow young Hegelians and Feuerbachians was a romantic concept with a preponderantly sexual connotation. It was the language of a group which made a protest of romantic individualism against the new capitalist civilization . . .' Feuer's assertion, however, that for Marx in 1844 'the sexual meaning of "alienation" was still central', is highly debatable. See text below.

5. K. Marx, *Manuscripts* (op. cit.), p. 85.

6. ibid., p. 76.

7. ibid., p. 139.

8. ibid., p. 102.

9. K. Marx and F. Engels, *The German Ideology* (1845), London, 1965, p. 37; selections, New York, 1970.

10. K. Marx and F. Engels, *Manifesto of the Communist Party* (op. cit.), p. 42.

11. K. Marx, *The Poverty of Philosophy* (1847), Moscow, n.d., p. 167.

12. *Manifesto* (op. cit.), p. 103.

13. ibid., p. 67.

14. *Poverty of Philosophy* (op. cit.), p. 65.

15. *Manifesto* (op. cit.), p. 50.

16. ibid., p. 63.

17. K. Marx, *A Contribution to the Critique of Political Economy* (1859), London and New York, 1971, p. 21 (Preface).

18. See, for example, Marx's Letter to Kugelman (1871) and his Amsterdam Speech (1872), in Shlomo Avineri, *The Social and Political Thought of Karl Marx*, London, 1968, and New York, 1971, p. 49; also Marx's Letter to Hyndman, in David McLellan, *Karl Marx: his life and thought*, London, 1973, and New York, 1974, p. 444.

19. G. D. H. Cole, *A History of Socialist Thought*, London and New York, 1954, Vol. II, p. 297.

20. K. Marx, *Capital*, Vol. I (1867), Moscow, 1961, p. 8 (Preface to the first German edn).

21. He wrote: 'If Marx did not leave behind him a "*Logic*" (with a capital letter), he did leave the *logic* of *Capital* . . . In *Capital*, Marx applied to a single science logic, dialectics and the theory of knowledge of material-

ism ... which has taken everything valuable in Hegel and developed it further.' (V. I. Lenin, *Collected Works*, Vol. 38 (Philosophical Notebooks), London, 1961, p. 319.)

22. This heavy tome of about a thousand pages was first published in Moscow in 1941, and in Berlin, by Dietz Verlag, in 1953. Although parts were translated into English before, the full text first appeared only in 1973, translated and with a very helpful Introduction by Martin Nicolaus (K. Marx, *Grundrisse: introduction to the critique of political economy*, New York, 1971, and Harmondsworth, 1973).

23. *Capital*, I (op. cit.), p. 71.

24. ibid., p. 208.

25. *Capital*, Vol. III (1894), Moscow, 1962, p. 798.

26. *Capital*, I (op. cit.), p. 233.

27. *Capital*, III (op. cit.), p. 254. In certain passages of the *Grundrisse* Marx goes even further in the direction of technological determinism. For example, with automation being achieved, Marx thinks that now 'the surplus-labour of the mass has ceased to be the condition for the development of general wealth, just as the non-labour of the few, for the development of the general powers of the human hand.' (op. cit., p. 705.)

28. *Capital*, I (op. cit.), p. 488.

29. ibid., p. 80.

30. ibid., p. 184.

31. *Capital*, III (op. cit.), p. 800.

32. *Contribution to the critique of political economy* (op. cit.), p. 21.

33. See, for example, *German Ideology* (op. cit.), p. 60; *Poverty of Philosophy* (op. cit.), p. 105.

34. *Manifesto* (op. cit.), p. 61. Cf. also: 'The working men have no country. We cannot take from them what they have not got.' (ibid., p. 76.)

35. Marx's earliest reference to this is in a Letter to Weydemeyer, 1852, where he claims to have proved 'that the class struggle necessarily leads to the dictatorship of the proletariat...' (reprinted in K. Marx, *The Eighteenth Brumaire of Louis Bonaparte* (1852), Moscow, n.d., p. 139). The phrase is also used in Marx's critical notes on the unity programme of German social democrats. See *Critique of the Gotha Programme* (1875), Moscow, n.d., p. 31.

36. On this point Marx always took a moderate, realistic view, even, which is sometimes overlooked by critics, in his youthful period when he thought that the arrival of communism 'will constitute in actual fact a very severe and protracted process.' (*Manuscripts* (op. cit.), p. 124.)

37. *Critique of the Gotha Programme* (op. cit.), p. 22.

38. The last of Marx's famous 'Theses on Feuerbach' (1845). See *German Ideology* (op. cit.), p. 647.

39. *Manuscripts* (op. cit.), p. 105.

40. ibid., p. 100.

41. *Manifesto* (op. cit.), p. 81.

42. ibid.

43. ibid., p. 71.

44. *Capital*, I (op. cit.), p. 330.

45. E. H. Carr, *Karl Marx: a study in fanaticism*, London, 1934, p. 83. Or consider the view of an eminent economist: '. . . no point of substance in Marx's argument depends upon the labour theory of value. Voltaire remarked that it is possible to kill a flock of sheep by witchcraft if you give them plenty of arsenic at the same time. The sheep, in this figure, may well stand for the complacent apologists of capitalism; Marx's penetrating insight and bitter hatred of oppression supply the arsenic, while the labour theory of value provides the incantations.' (Joan Robinson, *An Essay on Marxian Economics*, London, 1947, and New York, 1966, p. 22.) Cf. also Cole (op. cit.), p. 285 ff.

46. One would perhaps be entitled to argue that there never really was *one* Marxism, in the sense of a homogeneous movement inspired by a perfectly clear, transparent doctrine, even in the founder's life-time. It is well known that Marx quarrelled bitterly not only with rival socialist theorists, usually exaggerating their differences, but also with his own well-meaning disciples. He declared to Paul Lafargue, his son-in-law, in the 1880s that 'he was no Marxist', accusing at the same time some of his closest associates of 'Proudhonism' and 'Bakuninism'. See McLellan, *Karl Marx* (op. cit.), p. 443.

5. Ideas in Ferment and the Parting of the Ways

1. Talking about the origins of Fabianism, Shaw once said: 'To the Lassallian politics we have added only pure detail. Social Democracy, then, as a definite ideal and an intelligible and consistent policy, dates from the year 1862; and Lassalle must be regarded as its founder . . .' (G. B. Shaw, *The Road to Equality: Ten Unpublished Lectures and Essays 1884–1918*, Boston, 1971, p. 65.)

2. F. Lassalle, *Arbeiter-Programm* (1862), in *Sozialoekonomische Texte*, Frankfurt a.M., 1948, p. 49.

3. ibid., p. 47.

4. *Offenes Antwortschreiben an das Central Comite* (1863); ibid., p. 83.

5. John Saville, 'The Ideology of Labourism', in Benewick (op. cit.); p. 214.

6. G. Lichtheim, *Marxism: An Historical and Critical Study*, London, 1961, and New York, 1964; p. 212.

7. In later editions of his *Principles* Mill expressed cautiously sympathetic views on 'socialism' and 'communism', accepting them as viable alternatives to capitalism in a distant future. He considered, for example, that 'the restraints of communism would be freedom in comparison with the present condition of the majority of the human race'. His discussion of these subjects, however, is strictly 'academic' here and elsewhere. See J. S. Mill, *Principles of Political Economy with Some of their Applications to Social Philosophy* (7th edn, 1871), ed. and introduced by W. J. Ashley, London, 1923, p. 210 and ff.

8. *Report on Fabian Policy* (Fabian Tract No. 70), London, 1896, Par. XIV, p. 8.

9. Sydney Olivier on the 'moral basis' of socialism, in G. B. Shaw et al., *Fabian Essays* (1889), London, 1962, p. 138.

10. Sidney Webb on the 'historic basis' of socialism, ibid., p. 90.

11. *Report on Fabian Policy* (op. cit.), Par. XII, p. 7.

12. A random survey of the titles of some Fabian tracts in the early period shows this typically cool, empirical approach: Allotments and How to Get Them; Life in the Laundry; Municipal Bakeries; Municipal Pawnshops; Scandal of London's Markets; Sweating: its Cause and Remedy; Tenants' Sanitary Catechism, etc. etc.

13. G. K. Chesterton, *The Victorian Age in Literature*, London, 1912, p. 236.

14. See the recent analysis in Stanley Pierson, *Marxism and the Origins of British Socialism*, Ithaca, 1973, Part II, Ch. 6.

15. R. Blatchford, *Merrie England*, London, 1894, p. 12.

16. ibid., p. 15.

17. ibid., p. 72.

18. ibid., p. 99.

19. For the Marxist case, demolishing the 'myth' of Morris's moralism, see E. P. Thompson, *William Morris: Romantic to Revolutionary*, London, 1955, pp. 735–46, 892–9; R. Page Arnot, *William Morris: the Man and the Myth*, London, 1961. J. W. Hulse, however, emphasizes the similarity between Morris's and the anarchists' ideal of future society, suggesting that the anarchist writer Kropotkin inspired Morris's *News From Nowhere* (*Revolutionists in London: a study of five unorthodox socialists*, Oxford and New York, 1970, p. 89, p. 99). It is interesting to note that despite Morris's disclaimers in his political speeches, he showed himself distinctly uneasy regarding the anarchist future ideal. See for example the passages

in *News From Nowhere* where 'Old Hammond', asked by the 'Guest' about the tyranny of society in this utopia, 'bursts out laughing', but on the whole manages to evade the question. (*News From Nowhere*, ed. by J. Redmond, London and Boston, 1970, pp. 76–7.)

20. W. Morris, 'The Society of the Future' (1887), in *Political Writings*, ed. and introduced by A. R. Morton, London and New York, 1973, p. 192. More explicitly libertarian formulations are found, of course, in the case of many other English writers in the period. For example, Oscar Wilde's *The Soul of Man* (London, 1907) argues the identity of socialism and a most extreme kind of individualism; Edward Carpenter's *Towards Democracy* (London, 1905) preaches the primacy of sentiment and sexual liberation.

21. W. Morris, 'Socialism and Anarchism' (1889), ibid., p. 213.

22. W. Morris and E. Belfort Bax, *Socialism: its Growth and Outcome*, London, 1893, p. 298.

23. E. Belfort Bax, *The Ethics of Socialism, etc.*, London, 1902, pp. 28–30.

24. G. Woodcock, *Anarchism*, Harmondsworth and New York, 1962, p. 31. Cf. also: 'No conception of anarchism is farther from the truth than that which regards it as an extreme form of democracy. Democracy advocates the sovereignty of the people. Anarchism advocates the sovereignty of the person.' (ibid., p. 30.)

25. The reference is of course to Stirner's one shattering book-length manifesto, *Der Einzige und sein Eigenthum* (Leipzig, 1844), which has been given the misleading English title, *The Ego and His Own*. There are several American and British editions which are, however, not very easy to get hold of. See the recent 'Roots of the Right' series for a readily available though abridged edition, with a useful introduction by John Carroll (London and New York, 1971).

26. Though this is convincingly argued in the recent analysis, R. W. K. Paterson, *The Nihilistic Egoist: Max Stirner*, London and New York, 1971, p. 144.

27. It is instructive to see that Marx and Engels, in several hundred pages of closely argued 'conceptual analysis' of Stirner's book, never succeed in mounting a clear frontal attack on egoism, falling back instead on castigating Stirner's 'petty bourgeois' assumptions and his political quietism. As Paterson rightly remarks, Marx's 'heavy mockery fails to conceal his real and continuous anxiety lest his prey should finally prove invulnerable to his envenomed barbs.' (op. cit., p. 107.) And as Carroll argues, Marx and Engels showed 'an embarrassed reaction to the anarcho-hedonistic programme, with its attendant ludic principle, a reaction consistent with their evasive attitude to the entire domain of individualist psychology' (*Break-Out From the Crystal Palace*, op. cit. p. 82). Cf.

also D. McLellan, *The Young Hegelians and Karl Marx*, London and New York, 1969, pp. 130–5.

28. Cf. Nietzsche's contemptuous dismissal of 'glib-tongued and scribe-fingered slaves of the democratic taste', 'blunt honest fellows' who are 'not free, and are ludicrously superficial, especially in their innate partiality for seeing the cause of almost *all* human misery and failure in the old forms in which society has hitherto existed—a notion which happily inverts the truth entirely!' Nietzsche has particular antipathy reserved for those who assert 'equal rights' and want to end all suffering. *Beyond Good and Evil; Prelude to a Philosophy of the Future*, trans. by H. Zimmern, in F. Nietzsche, *Complete Works*, London, 1923, Vol. 12., pp. 58–59.

29. See Woodcock (op. cit.), p. 218.

30. P.-J. Proudhon, *What is Property? An Inquiry into the Principle of Right and of Government* (1840), trans. by Benjamin Tucker (first English edn, 1890), New York, 1966, p. 277.

31. ibid., p. 285.

32. ibid., p. 261.

33. ibid., p. 256.

34. M. Bakunin, *God and the State* (MS 1871), introduced by P. Avrich, New York, 1970, p. 28.

35. ibid., p. 25.

36. ibid., p. 79.

37. ibid., p. 80.

38. ibid., p. 59.

39. G. Plekhanov, *Anarchismus und Sozialismus*, Berlin, 1904 (2nd edn), p. 56.

40. See Max Nomad, 'The Anarchist Tradition', in M. M. Drachkovitch (ed.), *The Revolutionary Internationals 1864–1943*, Stanford, 1966, p. 71, p. 92.

41. Bakunin was more serious in his critique of Marx's 'authoritarianism', though referring mainly to the latter's handling of the International, as distinguished from basic social principles. Marx, in turn, did not at all take Bakunin seriously as a social theorist, but on the other hand strongly condemned the Russian's addiction to secret societies, justifiably anxious lest Bakunin should succeed in capturing the International. However, the reader may profitably peruse Maurice Cranston's imaginative reconstruction of the Marx-Bakunin 'debate', where Marx is made to say, giving concise expression to the whole issue: 'Freedom, as I see it, is the liberation of mankind; not the liberty of the individual.' (M. Cranston, *Political Dialogues*, London, 1968, p. 137.)

Socialism

42. P. Kropotkin, *The Conquest of Bread* (1913), ed. and introduced by P. Avrich, London, 1972, p. 68. It is only fair to point out here, however, that Kropotkin's arguments in favour of 'communism' are among the best constructed to be found in socialist literature. See ibid. ff. and his *Mutual Aid: a Factor in Evolution* (1902), a scholarly piece in which Kropotkin argues against individualism and Social Darwinism of the Spencer-Huxley variety.

43. Plekhanov (op. cit.), p. 71. See, however, Shaw's Fabian pamphlet (Fabian Tract No. 45, 1893), 'The Impossibilities of Anarchism', where Kropotkin is judged—with justice—as being really a 'democrat'.

44. K. Kautsky, *Das erfurter Programm in seiner grundsaetzlichen Teil*, Stuttgart, 1892, p. 166.

45. H. M. Hyndman, *The Historical Basis of Socialism in England*, London, 1883, p. 425.

46. Bertrand Russell, *Roads to Freedom: Socialism, Anarchism and Syndicalism*, London, 1920 (3rd edn), p. 12.

47. F. F. Ridley, *Revolutionary Syndicalism in France: the Direct Action of its Time*, London, 1970, and New York, 1971, p. 104.

48. Reprinted in John Gretton, *Students and Workers: An Analytical Account of Dissent in France, May–June 1968*, London, 1969, p. 168. Some anarchist thinkers, of course, were suspicious of syndicalism. Errico Malatesta, for example, warned against 'the authoritarian structure [of syndicalism] which is the cause of the evils which today we complain of . . .' (V. Richards (ed.), *Errico Malatesta: His Life and Ideas*, London, 1965, p. 122).

49. Quoted in Russell (op. cit.), p. 78. Pelloutier, strangely enough, was an 'intellectual' who nevertheless made a lasting impact on organized workers. He also died very young, at the age of 34, in 1901.

50. Tom Mann, *Memoirs*, London, 1923, p. 317. Let us here again quote a beautiful passage from Blatchford, who, without being a syndicalist, expresses the rationale behind syndicalism: 'During an election there are Tory and Liberal capitalists, and all of them are friends of the workers. During a strike there are no Tories and no Liberals among the employers. They are all capitalists and enemies of the workers.' (op. cit., p. 200.)

51. Mann (op. cit.) p. 324.

52. cf. '. . . the general strike must be taken as a whole and undivided, and the passage from capitalism to socialism conceived as a catastrophe, the development of which baffles description.' (Georges Sorel, *Reflections on Violence* (1806), trans. by T. E. Hulme and J. Roth, New York, 1961, p. 148.) Also: 'It is to violence that socialism owes those high ethical values by means of which it brings *salvation* to the modern world.'

168

(ibid. p. 249.) Sorel, a most disturbing thinker, derived his ideas from Proudhon, Marx and Bergsonian 'life-force' philosophy. It was not entirely illogical from his point of view that he should have become a philosophical progenitor of Italian fascism.

53. See S. V. Utechin, *Russian Political Thought: A Concise History*, New York, 1964, p. 128.

54. Quoted in M. Prawdin, *The Unmentionable Nechaev: A Key to Bolshevism*, London, 1961, p. 63.

55. Quoted in A. L. Weeks, *The First Bolshevik: A Political Biography of Peter Tkachev*, New York, 1968, p. 173.

56. ibid., p. 94.

57. ibid., p. 101.

6. *Moralism: The Way of Western Social Democracy*

1. J. Jaures, *Studies in Socialism*, trans. and introduced by M. Minturn, London, 1908, p. 97.

2. E. Bernstein, *Evolutionary Socialism (Die Voraussetzungen des Sozialismus und die Aufgaben der Sozialdemokratie*, 1899), trans. by E. C. Harvey, introduced by S. Hook, New York, 1963, pp. 146-9.

3. See E. F. M. Durbin, *The Politics of Democratic Socialism: An Essay on Social Policy*, London and Clifton, N.J., 1940, pp. 125-33; C. A. R. Crosland, *The Future of Socialism*, London and New York, 1963 (revised edn), Part I, passim.

4. A. Bevan, *In Place of Fear*, London, 1952, p. 118.

5. See S. Haseler, *The Gaitskellites: Revisionism in the British Labour Party 1951-64*, London, 1969, Appendix II, p. 267; also in Harold Wilson, *The Relevance of British Socialism*, London, 1964, pp. 7-9.

6. Roy Jenkins, *What Matters Now*, London, 1972, pp. 21-2.

7. Social democrats in Britain, at any rate, have never moved away from the principle eloquently formulated by R. H. Tawney, for whom the object of socialism 'is to extend those [i.e. democratic] principles from the sphere of civil and political rights, where, at present, they are nominally recognized, to that of economic and social organization, where they are systematically and insolently defied. The socialist movement and the Labour Party exist for that purpose.' (*Equality* (1931), with a new introduction by R. M. Titmuss, London and New York, 1964, p. 197.)

8. Durbin, op. cit., p. 237.

9. ibid., p. 243.

10. Bernstein, op. cit., p. 151.

11. *Grundsatzprogramm der Sozialdemokratischen Partei Deutschlands,* Bonn, 1959.

12. Ralph Miliband, *Parliamentary Socialism: A Study in the Politics of Labour* (1961), second edn, London, 1973, p. 333.

13. Socialist Union, *Socialism: A New Statement of Principles*, London, 1952, pp. 30–1.

14. '. . . I am sure that a definite limit exists to the degree of equality which is desirable. We do not want complete equality of incomes, since extra responsibility and exceptional talent require and deserve a differential reward.' Crosland (op. cit.), p. 149.

15. ibid. p. 355. Crosland, consciously reacting to the 'Fabian tradition' of social democracy, argues for 'a greater emphasis on private life, on freedom and dissent, on culture, beauty, leisure, and even frivolity. Total abstinence and a good filing-system are not now the right signposts to the Socialist Utopia; or at least, if they are, some of us will fall by the wayside.' (ibid., p. 357.)

16. This is excellently argued in J. Gyford and S. Haseler, *Social Democracy: Beyond Revisionism*, London, Fabian Society (Research Series 292), 1971.

17. '*This is SAP*', Stockholm (Swedish Social Democratic Labour Party), 1953, p. 8. As an historian has noted, in the 1960s the Swedish welfare state was 'still very much a society of class differences'. (Kurt Samuelsson, *From Great Power to Welfare State: 300 Years of Swedish Social Development*, London and New York, 1968, p. 283.)

18. '*This is SAP*' (op. cit.), p. 25.

19. In the light of the ancestry of social democracy, it is interesting to note that Swedish industry, notably the Saab-Scania and Volvo car manufacturing concerns, has pioneered with experiments in job rotation and the abolition of the monotony of the 'production line'.

20. Henri de Man, *The Psychology of Socialism* (1926), trans. from the 2nd German edn by E. and C. Paul, London, 1928, p. 417.

21. Cf. 'In an era when most leftist parties in Western democracies are moderating or abandoning their old ideologies, the French Socialists remain dedicated to their Marxist ideology.' (F. L. Wilson, *The French Democratic Left 1963–1969: Toward a Modern Party System*, Stanford, 1971.)

22. K. Kautsky, *Terrorismus und Kommunismus*, Berlin, 1919, p. 135. See also K. Kautsky, *Von der Demokratie zur Staats-Sklaverei. Eine Auseinandersetzung mit Trotzki*, Berlin, 1921.

23. R. H. S. Crossman, 'Towards a Philosophy of Socialism', in A. Albu et al., *New Fabian Essays* (1952), London, 1970, p. 12. Cf. also Socialist Union, op. cit., p. 19.

24. Bevan, op. cit., p. 169.
25. Cf. W. E. Paterson and T. Campbell, *Social Democracy in Post-War Europe*, London, 1974, p. 64.
26. Bevan, op. cit., p. 168.
27. Durbin, op. cit., p. 288.
28. ibid.
29. Salvador Allende, although a committed Marxist ('Our objective is total, scientific, Marxist socialism'), apparently believed that he could pull through without a civil war. See Régis Debray, *Conversations with Allende: Socialism in Chile*, London, 1971. For analyses of the army coup and its aftermath, see Ralph Miliband, 'The Coup in Chile', 'Socialist Register', 1973; Helios Prieto, *Chile: the Gorillas are among us*, London, 1974.
30. Cf. '. . . it is a tragedy that in the world conflict of the super-powers and their ideologies the way of Democratic Socialism tends to be despised or ignored.' (Albert Carthy, 'The Socialist International in Perspective', in *The Socialist International: A Short History*, London, 1969.)
31. M. Harrington, *Socialism*, New York, 1970, p. 189.

7. *Rationalism: The European Marxist Establishment*

1. V. I. Lenin, *What is to be done?* (1902), trans. by V. and P. Utechin, London, 1970, p. 80.
2. V. I. Lenin, *One Step Forward, Two Steps Back: The Crisis in our Party* (1904), *Collected Works*, Moscow, 1961, Vol. 7, p. 269. It was also in this tract that Lenin defined 'revolutionary social democracy' in terms of 'Jacobinism' (p. 383). In 1918, of course, Lenin renamed his Bolshevik faction of the Russian Social Democratic Party as the 'Communist Party' in order to distinguish his line more sharply from what he called 'opportunism'.
3. ibid., p. 389.
4. ibid.
5. V. I. Lenin, *The State and Revolution* (1918), *Collected Works*, Moscow, 1964, Vol. 25, p. 426.
6. ibid., p. 430.
7. V. I. Lenin, *Imperialism, the highest stage of capitalism* (1918), *Collected Works*, Moscow, 1964, Vol. 22, p. 226.
8. L. Trotsky, *The Permanent Revolution* (1929), New York, 3rd edn, 1969, p. 146.
9. ibid., p. 276.

10. See the stimulating discussion in N. Krassò, 'Trotsky's Marxism', 'New Left Review', No. 44, July–August, 1967, and the reply by a leading Trotskist theorist, E. Mandel, 'Trotsky's Marxism: an Anti-Critique', 'New Left Review', No. 47, Jan.–Feb., 1968.

11. Russia was in 1917 and remained for a long time an overwhelmingly agricultural country with the industrial working class constituting a small minority of the population. Cf. 'The Leninist state was therefore a dictatorship of the proletariat, for the proletariat, but not by the proletariat, or, as Otto Bauer phrased it, a "dictatorship of the idea of the proletariat".' (A. G. Meyer, *Leninism*, Cambridge, Mass., 1957, p. 208.)

12. E. H. Carr, *1917: Before and After*, London, 1969, and New York, 1971, p. 154.

13. L. Trotsky, *Their Morals and Ours* (1938), New York, 1972, p. 25.

14. *Trotsky's Diary in Exile 1935*, trans. by E. Zarodnaya, London, 1959, p. 38.

15. Even as staunch a critic of Stalinism as Roy Medvedev admits that Stalin 'did enjoy the confidence of a majority of the Party and the people'. (R. A. Medvedev, *Let History Judge: the Origins and Consequences of Stalinism*, London, 1971, and New York, 1972, p. 564.)

16. Sidney and Beatrice Webb, chief proponents of rationalism in its Fabian variety, wrote that what 'induced' them primarily to embark on their investigation of the Soviet Union was 'the deliberate planning of all the nation's production, distribution and exchange, not for swelling the profit of the few but for increasing the consumption of the whole community'. (S. and B. Webb, *Soviet Communism: a New Civilization?*, London, 1935, p. 602.)

17. I. V. Stalin, *Report to the 17th Congress of the C.P.S.U.(b) 1934*, in *The Essential Stalin: Major Theoretical Writings 1905–52*, ed. and introduced by B. Franklin, New York, 1972, and London, 1973, p. 280.

18. ibid., p. 280.

19. I. V. Stalin, *Economic Problems of Socialism in the U.S.S.R.* (1952), in ibid., p. 459. Talking about the growing inequality in state socialism, a recent analysis has pointed out: 'In the U.S.S.R. Stalin by virtue of his administrative control implemented such changes, whereas in Eastern Europe it is the self-styled anti-Stalinists who have called for greater reliance on market mechanisms, financial incentives and the abolition of the "damaging levelling of wages".' (D. Lane, *The End of Inequality? Stratification under state socialism*, Harmondsworth, 1971, p. 76.)

20. *Economic Problems*, in Stalin (op. cit.), p. 476.

21. R. C. Tucker, *The Marxian Revolutionary Idea*, New York, 1969, and London, 1970, p. 202.

22. *The New Soviet Society* (Final Text of the Programme of the C.P.S.U., 1961), introduced by H. Ritvo, New York, 1962, p. 167.

23. I. Deutscher, *Ironies of History: Essays on Contemporary Communism*, London, 1966, and Palo Alto, Calif., 1971, p. 139.

24. *The New Soviet Society* (op. cit.), p. 110.

25. ibid.

26. ibid., p. 112.

27. ibid., p. 154.

28. See L. Smolinski, 'Towards a Socialist Corporation: Soviet Industrial Reorganization of 1973', *Survey*, Vol. 20, No. 1, Winter, 1974.

29. Quoted in F. Fejto, *A History of the People's Democracies: Eastern Europe Since Stalin*, trans. by D. Weissbart, New York, 1971, p. 143. Yugoslavia, according to another observer, has had to cope with 'the heritage of Stalinism and the birth-pangs of capitalism' (ibid., p. 332). Cf. also L. Sirc, *Economic Devolution in Eastern Europe*, London, 1969, pp. 134–143.

30. Fejto (op. cit.), pp. 150–4.

31. Cf. Lane's conclusion: 'A state-socialist society is above all a technical-administrative society, where man's social position is increasingly determined by education, qualifications and technical-administrative performance.' (op. cit., p. 135.) A recent observer in Eastern Europe has ventured even further, predicting the eventual demise of the 'party' itself: 'As specialists take over one specialized function after another, and as each new generation becomes better at managing for itself, so the state, while remaining a live body, will cease to have any room for the Party at its centre.' (P. Neuburg, *The Hero's Children: The Postwar Generation in Eastern Europe*, London, 1972, and New York, 1973, p. 361.) Cf., however, the perceptive analysis in S. White, 'Contradiction and Change in State Socialism', *Soviet Studies*, Vol. XXVI, No. 1, Jan. 1974.

32. de Man (op. cit.), p. 220.

33. Cf. the Maoist critique: 'Before the October Revolution, tsarist Russia was a "paradise" where many Western capitalist countries exported capital, reaped colossal profits and plundered industrial raw materials. Today, 50 years later, the Soviet revisionist leaders once again allow the monopoly capitalist groups of these countries to reach their claws into the Soviet land.' (*How the Soviet Revisionists Carry Out All-Round Restoration of Capitalism in the U.S.S.R.*, Peking, 1968, p. 6.)

34. E. G. Liberman, 'The Plan, Profits and Bonuses' (1962), reprinted in A. Nove and D. M. Nuti (eds), *Socialist Economics*, Harmondsworth, 1972, p. 314.

35. See Fejto, op. cit., p. 143; D. Plamenic, 'The Belgrade Student Insurrec-

tion', 'New Left Review', No. 54, March–April 1959. The most striking statement of left-wing-egalitarian criticism of East European developments is in J. Kuron and K. Modzelewski, *An Open Letter to the Party* (1964), London, n.d. For an example of moderate, 'super-rationalist' criticism, see A. Sakharov, *et al.*, 'Appeal for a Gradual Democratization' (Letter to Soviet leaders, 1970), reprinted in G. Saunders (ed.), *Samizdat: Voices of the Soviet Opposition*, New York, 1974, pp. 399–412.

36. An indication that East European 'humanist' Marxist philosophers appreciate this difficulty is the recent analysis by S. Stojanovic, *Between Ideals and Reality: A Critique of Socialism and its Future*, trans. by G. S. Sher, New York, 1973. Although remaining essentially starry-eyed and further developing the Djilas thesis on the 'new class' in state socialism, Stojanovic notes the difference between a Maoist egalitarian critique and the humanistic, libertarian New Left (see p. 74).

8. *Egalitarianism: The Lean and Hungry Socialists*

1. A surprisingly high-handed attitude is displayed, for example, by George Lichtheim, who calls Maoism the 'infantile parody of Lenin's thought' and rebukes the Cubans for relying on 'Jacobin rhetoric'. See *A Short History of Socialism* (op. cit.), p. 282, p. 284.

2. See the discussion in Chapter Four ('From Proletarianism to Modernizing Movement') of J. H. Kautsky's *Communism and the Politics of Development: Persistent Myths and Changing Behaviour*, New York, 1968.

3. Tom Mboya, 'African Socialism', Appendix IV. W. H. Friedland and C. G. Rosberg, Jr. (eds), *African Socialism*, Stanford, Calif., 1964, p. 251; Julius K. Nyerere, 'Ujamaa: the basis of African socialism', ibid., Appendix II, p. 246; Leopold S. Senghor, *On African Socialism*, trans. by M. Cook, London, 1964, p. 72. Cf. also A. M. Said and M. S. Ahmed, *Arab Socialism*, London and New York, 1972.

4. Frantz Fanon, *Toward the African Revolution* (1964), trans. by H. Chevalier, Harmondsworth, 1970, pp. 154–5; New York, 1968.

5. Frantz Fanon, *The Wretched of the Earth* (1961), trans. by C. Farrington, Preface by J.-P. Sartre, Harmondsworth, 1967, p. 73; New York, 1965.

6. ibid., p. 37.

7. ibid., p. 89.

8. ibid., p. 103.

9. Mao Tse-tung, *Selected Works*, Peking, 1967, Vol. I, p. 32.

10. Stuart S. Schram, *The Political Thought of Mao Tse-tung*, revised edn, Harmondsworth, 1969, p. 78; New York, 1969.

11. See Speech by L. I. Brezhnyev, June, 1969. ('Current Digest of the Soviet Press', Vol. XXI, No. 23, p. 11.) It is of some interest to note that moderate internal critics of the Soviet system often echo or even accentuate the 'official' accusations. Medvedev, for example, denounces 'the monstrous crimes' of the Chinese leaders (op. cit., p. 562), while Sakharov warns against the danger of 'Chinese totalitarian nationalism' (Saunders, op. cit., p. 411).

12. See the discussion by Deutscher in *Ironies of History* (op. cit.), 'Maoism —its origins and outlook', esp. pp. 110–19.

13. Schram (op. cit.), p. 350.

14. *Selected Works* (op. cit.), Vol. III, p. 119.

15. ibid., Vol. I, p. 108. See the excellent discussion on the connection between Maoism and classical European egalitarianism in B. I. Schwartz, 'The Reign of Virtue: Some Broad Perspectives on Leader and Party in the Cultural Revolution', *China Quarterly*, 35, July–Sept., 1968.

16. *Selected Works*, Vol. II, p. 31.

17. ibid., p. 32.

18. ibid., p. 198.

19. Mao Tse-tung, *On the Correct Handling of Contradictions Among the People* (1956), Peking, 1966, p. 6.

20. ibid., p. 32.

21. Mao Tse-tung, *Speech at the Chinese Communist Party's National Conference on Propaganda Work* (1957), Peking, p. 6.

22. See Schram (op. cit.), p. 143. In China, apparently, premarital sexual relations are rare and socially unacceptable. In the words of a recent observer: 'To an American visitor, a sexless society up to the middle twenties—even when combined with hard work, social pressure and total political commitment—seems a remarkable phenomenon.' (C. Djerassi, 'Some Observations on Current Fertility Control in China', *China Quarterly*, 57, Jan.–March, 1974.) For a sympathetic appreciation of Chinese 'puritanism' by a Western socialist writer, see Sheila Rowbotham, *Women, Resistance and Revolution*, London, 1972, and New York, 1973, p. 193.

23. *Selected Works*, Vol. I, p. 318.

24. Schram (op. cit.), p. 304.

25. *On the Correct Handling of Contradictions* (op. cit.), p. 3. See also Schram (op. cit.), p. 97.

26. See, for example, J. Gerassi (ed.), *Revolutionary Priest: The Complete Writings and Messages of Camillo Torres* (1971), Harmondsworth, 1973; Helder Camara, *Structures of Injustice*, London, 1972; G. Gutierrez, *A Theology of Liberation*, New York, 1973.

27. Régis Debray, *Revolution in the Revolution?* (Harmondsworth, 1968). Debray's thesis, understandably, earned him many critics representing the orthodox Marxist, including Maoist, point of view. See Cecil Johnson, *Communist China and Latin America 1959–1967*, New York, 1970, pp. 173–7.

28. Debray, op. cit., p. 69, p. 113.

29. See R. M. Bernardo, *The Theory of Moral Incentives in Cuba*, Alabama, 1971, p. 58.

30. Cecil Johnson (op. cit.), p. 159.

31. Ernesto Che Guevara, *Venceremos! The Speeches and Writings of Che Guevara*, ed. by J. Gerassi, London, 1968, and New York, 1969, p. 421.

32. ibid., p. 343.

33. ibid., p. 304.

34. ibid., p. 148.

35. ibid., p. 311.

36. ibid., p. 175.

37. ibid., p. 162.

38. ibid., p. 541.

39. ibid., p. 296.

40. ibid., p. 551.

41. Fidel Castro, *Major Speeches 1965–1968* (Stenographic Dept of the Revolutionary Government), London, 1968, p. 273.

42. Bernardo (op. cit.) p. 56.

43. ibid., p. 126.

44. I. L. Horowitz (ed.), *Cuban Communism*, New York, 1970, p. 18.

45. R. Dumont, *Is Cuba Socialist?*, trans. by S. Hochman, London, 1973, p. 112.

46. Bernardo (op. cit.), p. 119.

47. See R. P. Appelbaum, *Theories of Social Change*, Chicago, 1970, pp. 36–59, for a discussion of contemporary 'evolutionary' theories. Cf. also A. G. Frank, *Sociology of Development and Underdevelopment of Sociology*, London, 1971.

48. Cf. 'The patriotism of the Chinese, which runs very deep, is so completely fused with socialist ideology that they do not notice that there is a national element in it.' (Joan Robinson, *The Cultural Revolution in China*, Harmondsworth, 1970, p. 40.)

49. See Bernardo (op. cit.), p. 137. Cf. also P. Clecak, 'Moral and Material Incentives', 'Socialist Register', 1969, pp. 101–35.

9. *Libertarianism: The Love-Makers*

1. The term 'New Left' has many connotations. In Britain it is often used to denote writers associated with the influential 'New Left Review' and other prominent intellectuals like Raymond Williams and E. P. Thompson. The socialism of this 'New Left' consists in anti-Stalinist Marxism combined with the resurrection of certain aspects of the native British socialist tradition, carrying also some amount of libertarian influence. See concluding paragraphs of text.

2. C. Reich, *The Greening of America*, New York, 1970, and London, 1971, p. 262.

3. The point that today's genuine 'revolutionary' impetus originates in the United States is argued convincingly in J.-F. Revel, *Without Marx or Jesus: the New American Revolution Has Begun* (New York, 1971, and London, 1972), an otherwise most unsatisfactory and pointless book. Mary McCarthy in her 'Afterword', though very critical of Revel's approach, yet admits that the following New Left concerns did in fact come from America; Draft Refusal, Dropping Out, Woodstock, Drug Culture, Panthers, Women's Lib, Yippies, concern about the environment, the back-to-nature movement (p. 209).

4. See D. E. Apter and J. Joll (eds), *Anarchism Today* (London, 1971, and New York, 1972), especially pp. 35–58, where M. Lerner draws up an extensive list of recent libertarian attitudes coming straight out of the tradition of European anarchism.

5. Quoted in W. Reich, *The Sexual Revolution* (1944), trans. by T. P. Wolfe, London, 1951, p. 188.

6. A. Kollontai, *Love and the New Morality* (1919), reprinted with *Sexual Relations and the Class Struggle*, trans. by A. Holt, Bristol, 1972, p. 16.

7. W. Reich, *Sex-Pol: Essays 1929–1934,* ed. by L. Baxandall, New York, 1972, p. 19.

8. ibid., p. 51n.

9. See esp. the Preface to W. Reich, *The Function of the Orgasm* (1942), trans. by T. P. Wolfe, London, 1968.

10. Cf. 'The abolition of the commodity economy necessarily brings about the elimination of sexual morality and replaces it on a scientifically higher and technically more secure level with sex-economic regulation and support for sexual activity.' (*Sex-Pol* (op. cit.), p. 242.)

11. Reich, at one point, connected heterosexuality to revolutionary ideas and homosexuality to right-wing inclinations. See *Sex-Pol* (op. cit.), p. 297, and W. Reich, *The Sexual Struggle of Youth* (1931), London, 1972, where homosexuality is squarely denounced as 'abnormal' (pp. 49–52).

12. See M. Jay, *The Dialectical Imagination*, London and Boston, Mass., 1973, pp. 57–8, pp. 174–215; G. Rohrmoser, *Das Elend der kritischen Theorie*, Freiburg, 1970, pp. 68–70.

13. H. Marcuse, *One-Dimensional Man*, Boston, Mass., 1964, and London, 1968, p. 35.

14. H. Marcuse, *Eros and Civilization: A Philosophical Inquiry into Freud*, Boston, Mass., 1955, and London, 1972, p. 163.

15. H. Marcuse, 'Liberation from the Affluent Society', in D. Cooper (ed.), *Dialectics of Liberation*, 1968, p. 184.

16. H. Marcuse, *An Essay on Liberation*, London, and Boston, Mass., 1969, p. 21.

17. In many of his books, articles and interviews, particularly the harsh-toned essay on *Repressive Tolerance*, Marcuse takes a more explicitly political, egalitarian line. The discontinuities and dilemmas of his thought, being representative of the wider split in the New Left, are criticized at greater length in R. N. Berki, 'Marcuse and the crisis of the new radicalism: from politics to religion?', 'The Journal of Politics', Vol. 34, No. 1, Feb. 1972.

18. K. Millett, *Sexual Politics* (1970), London and New York, 1971, p. 25.

19. ibid., p. 62.

20. ibid., p. 169.

21. ibid., p. 362.

22. G. Greer, *The Female Eunuch*, London, 1971, and New York, 1972, p. 329.

23. ibid.

24. ibid., p. 299.

25. ibid., p. 316.

26. ibid., p. 302.

27. ibid., p. 317.

28. ibid., p. 20.

29. ibid., p. 326.

30. J. Mitchell, *Psychoanalysis and Feminism*, London, 1974, p. 416. Cf. also, ibid., p. 200, p. 222, pp. 383–98.

31. S. Rowbotham, *Women, Resistance and Revolution*. London, 1972, and New York, 1973, p. 245.

32. ibid., p. 218. Cf. a recent report from Cuba: 'Critical U.S. women's liberationists are interested in knowing the degree to which Cuban women see themselves as a group. In talking with Cuban women about this, it becomes clear that they see themselves primarily as Cuban revolu-

tionaries—and secondarily as women.' (Chris Camarano, 'On Cuban Women', 'Science and Society', Vol. XXXV, No. 1, Spring 1971.)

33. S. Rowbotham, *Woman's Consciousness, Man's World*, Harmondsworth, 1973, p. 22.

34. R. Neville, *Play Power*, London and New York, 1971, p. 207.

35. D. and G. Cohn-Bendit, *Obsolete Communism: The Leftwing Alternative*, trans. by A. Pomerans, Harmondsworth, 1968, and New York, 1969, p. 255. The authors conclude: 'There is only one reason for being a revolutionary—because it is the best way to live.' Cf. Neville: 'What about the workers? They're not fooled by the rantings of obsequious students. They know the revolution's done for fun—not them. And anyway, they hate the dirt and hair and polysyllables.' (op. cit., p. 207.)

36. Neville (op. cit.), p. 37.

37. Cf. the West German symposium, Diethart Krebs (ed.), *Die hedonistische Linke*, Neuwied, 1970, where the 'hedonistic Left' (i.e. libertarianism) is seen to be on its way to the creation of the 'free Ghetto'. Revel reports some practical jokers in Berlin in the 60s, who quoted anonymously Mussolini on the virtue of renouncing the 'easy life' to New Left student audiences—to the applause of the crowd (op. cit., p. 184).

38. The Broadway hit, 'Che', was described by its author 'as a political statement in dramatic guise, the presentation of an allegorical conflict between the President of the United States, a CIA agent, a Roman Catholic nun, and Guevara in terms of uninhibited sexual aggression' (quoted in L. Graham, *No More Morals: The Sexual Revolution*, New York, 1971, p. 200). It may be relevant to note here one of Fidel Castro's statements in conversation on homosexuality: '. . . we would never come to believe that a homosexual could embody the conditions and require-ments of conduct that would enable us to consider him a true Revolu-tionary, a true Communist militant. A deviation of that nature clashes with the concept we have of what a militant Communist must be . . . (quoted in Rowbotham, *Women, Resistance and Revolution*, op. cit., p. 231).

39. Quoted in Graham (op. cit.), p. 81.

40. T. Leary, *The Politics of Ecstasy* (1965), New York, 1968, and London, 1970, p. 140.

41. ibid., p. 133.

42. ibid., p. 59.

43. Neville (op. cit.), p. 114.

44. Graham (op. cit.), p. 128.

45. Neville reports, hailing this as a sign of the 'fun-loving' rebels' ascen-dancy, the 1969 May Day Appeal issued by the *Socialist Worker*, in

Socialism

which workers are invited to an open-air pop festival instead of a political demonstration (op. cit., p. 209).

46. Cf. Marcuse, *One-Dimensional Man*, op. cit., p. 73; R. Reiche, *Sexuality and Class Struggle* (1968), trans. by S. Bennett, London, 1970, p. 106; Rowbotham, *Woman's Consciousness, Man's World*, op. cit., pp. 113–114.

47. *Sunday Times Magazine*, 9.12.1973. Cf. also Peter Sedgwick on R. D. Laing, in *The Listener*, Vol. 87, No. 2251, 18.5.1972.

48. W. Harich, 'Zur Kritik der revolutionären Ungeduld', 'Kursbuch', No. 19, 1969, p. 110.

Select Bibliography of General and Historical Works

J. BRAUNTHAL, *History of the International 1864–1914* (1961), trans. by H. Collins and K. Mitchell, London, 1966.

J. CARROLL, *Break-Out From the Crystal Palace*, London, 1974.

G. D. H. COLE, *History of Socialist Thought*, 7 vols, London, 1953–.

L. DERFLER, *Socialism since Marx: a Century of the European Left*, London and New York, 1973.

E. DURKHEIM, *Socialism and Saint-Simon* (1929), trans. by C. Sattler, Kent, Ohio, 1958, and London, 1959.

A. FRIED AND R. SANDERS (eds), *Socialist Thought: A Documentary History*, Edinburgh and New York, 1964.

A. GRAY, *The Socialist Tradition: Moses to Lenin*, London, 1946, and New York, 1968.

M. HARRINGTON, *Socialism*, New York, 1970.

E. HYAMS, *The Millennium Postponed: Socialism from Sir Thomas More to Mao Tse-tung*, London and New York, 1974.

R. KILROY-SILK, *Socialism Since Marx*, London and New York, 1972.

G. LICHTHEIM, *The Origins of Socialism*, London and New York, 1969.

G. LICHTHEIM, *A Short History of Socialism*, London and New York, 1970.

D. MCLELLAN, *Karl Marx: His Life and Thought*, London, 1973, and New York, 1974.

H. DE MAN, *The Psychology of Socialism* (1926), trans. by E. and C. Paul, London, 1928.

A. G. MEYER, *Leninism*, Cambridge, Mass., 1957.

M. SALVADORI (ed.), *Modern Socialism*, London and New York, 1968.

J. A. SCHUMPETER, *Capitalism, Socialism and Democracy*, London and New York, 1943.

H. SMITH, *The Economics of Socialism Reconsidered*, London, 1962.

J. L. TALMON, *The Origins of Totalitarian Democracy*, New York, 1961.

G. WOODCOCK, *Anarchism*, Harmondsworth and New York, 1962.

Index